Qur'anic Teachings in a Nutshell
Worldview, Ethics and Laws

Compiled and Translated by

Sheikh Yaqub Jafari
&
Ali Quli Qarai

First Edition 2021

ISBN: 9798777232335 (Hardcover)
ISBN: 978-1-955725-01-9 (Paperback)
ISBN: 9781955725064 (Epub edition)

© Sheikh Yaqub Jafari, Ali Quli Qarai, 2021

All rights reserved.
No part of this publication may be reproduced in any form,
or by any means, without written permission of the publisher.

First Published by
Tarjuman-e Wahy Cultural Institute

Contents

Preface 9

PART ONE
WORLDVIEW AND DOCTRINE

CHAPTER 1

Reason and Revelation 13

   Rationality as the Basis of Belief 13
   Revelation as the Source of Guidance 14

CHAPTER 2

Knowing God 19

   The Signs of God's Existence 19
   The Oneness of God 21
   God's Names and Attributes 25
   God, the All-Beneficent and the All-Merciful 26
   The Forgiver of Sins 28

CHAPTER 3

The Human Being in the Qur'an 31

   Man, God's Viceroy on Earth 31
   Human Nature 34
   Human dignity 35
   Man on the Path of Evolution 36
   Human Life a Test and Trial 38
   Divine Traditions in History 40
   Factors of the Fall of Societies 42

Freedom of Choice	44
The Conflict Between Right and Wrong	46
The Reign of the Righteous as the Final End of History	48

Chapter 4
The Role of God's Envoys — 50

The Prophets as God's Emissaries	50
Attributes of the Prophets	52
The Covenant of the Prophets	54
Humanity of the Prophets	55
God's Help to the Prophets	56
The Prophet's Proofs and Arguments	57
Mockery and Persecution of the Prophets	60
The Prophetic Mission	61
The Teachings of the Prophets	62
Enemies of the Prophets and Gainsayers	64
Miracles of the Prophets	65

Chapter 5
Prophet Muhammad — 68

The Qur'an on the Prophecies in Torah & the Gospel	68
Prophet Muhammad in the Hebrew Bible	70
Prophet Muhammad in the New Testament	78
Prophet Muhammad in the Qur'an	81
The Principles of His Invitation	82
The Prophet's Morals	85
Names and Titles of the Prophet in the Qur'an	86
Divine Help in the Prophet's life	88
The Obligation to Obey the Prophet	89
Spiritual Strengthening of the Prophet	91
The Prophet is to be Treated with Honour	93

CHAPTER 6
The Qur'an — 96

- The Greatness of the Qur'an — 96
- Revelation of the Qur'an — 98
- Recitation of the Qur'an — 100
- The Qur'an as Guidance — 101
- The Qur'an Confirms the Former Scriptures — 103
- Comprehensiveness of the Qur'an — 105

CHAPTER 7
Communities and Groups — 107

- The Emergence of Communities & Role of the Prophets — 107
- The Visage of the Faithful and the Faithless — 108
- The Faithful and the Godwary — 108
- The Faithless and the Evildoers — 111
- Non-Muslim Communities — 114
- Relations with Non-Muslims — 116
- The People of the Book: Jews and Christians — 118
- Israelites/Jews — 120
- Christians — 125

CHAPTER 8
Eschatology: Resurrection & Afterlife — 130

- God's Ability to Raise the Dead — 130
- The Day of Resurrection — 132
- The Gathering of People at the Resurrection — 133
- People's State at Resurrection — 134
- Doomsday Terror — 135
- Fair Rewards and Punishments — 137
- The Inhabitants of Paradise — 139
- The Inmates of Hell — 142

Part Two
The Ethics of the Qur'an

CHAPTER 9
Values and Norms: Individual and Social   147

    Faith and Righteous Conduct   147
    Knowledge, Awareness and Thought   149
    Repentance From Sin   151
    The Invitation to Virtues   153
    Trust in God   154
    Remembrance and Supplication   156
    Thanksgiving   157
    Self-Cultivation and Godwariness   159
    Patience and Perseverance   161
    Loving God's Friends, the Role Models   162
    Forgiving Others' Trespasses and Faults   164
    Gentleness in Behaviour and Polite Speech   165
    Sympathetic Advice and Good Faith   166
    Cooperation and Teamwork   167
    Respect for Others' Privacy   168
    Strengthening the Family System   169
    The Etiquette of Speaking and Listening; Disinformation   172
    Humility and Good Morals   173
    Greeting Others   175
    Cleanliness and Tidy Appearance   176

Part Three
The Laws of the Qur'an

CHAPTER 10
Obligations and Ordinances   181

    Obedience to God and the Apostle   182
    Learning the Laws   183

Justice and Fairness	185
Duty to Urge Rightful & Forbid Wrongful Conduct	187
Consultation	189
Loyalty to Trusts and Agreements	189
Sincerity and Intent of Nearness to God	190
Prayer and Fasting	192
Zakāt and Khums	196
The Ka'bah and the Holy Mosque	197
The Rites of Hajj	199
Goodness to Parents	201
The Rights of Neighbours and Relatives	202
War and Peace	203
Fulfilment of Vows and Oaths	205
Observance of Modesty and Norms of Decency	206

CHAPTER 11

Religious Prohibitions — 208

Polytheism and Hypocrisy	208
Homicide	210
Illicit Gains	211
Defamation and Lying	213
Backbiting, Vilification, Suspicion, and Spying	214
Adultery and Prostitution	215
Wine and Gambling	216
Theft, Banditry and Terrorism	217
Pursuit of Base Desires	218
Following the Devil	219
Vicious Conduct and Traits	221
Attending Sinful Gatherings	224

Index — 225

Preface

The Holy Qur'an is for Muslims the most reliable source for a correct understanding of the teachings of Islam and knowledge of this religion. The comprehensiveness of the Qur'an, which includes topics such as the origin of the human race, the purpose of creation, the missions of the prophets and their accounts, resurrection and afterlife, ethical teachings and norms, as well as laws and precepts governing individual and social conduct, and many other topics besides, is such as to satisfy every human being's thirst for revealed knowledge in a world bewildered by materialist worldviews.

Although the Arabic Qur'an is the most widely read and recited of books throughout the Muslim world, its teaching and message are not accessible to the great majority of non-Arab Muslims except through the medium of translation. Even in languages which have competent translations of the whole Qur'an, topically arranged selections of translated verses can be most helpful as vital aids to a better understanding of Islamic teachings on various issues.

In addition to works that introduce non-Muslims readers to the role of the Qur'an in the formation of Islamic culture and spirituality and those which describe its major themes, topical selections of verses and passages are also useful to make the book's contents accessible to many readers who lack the time and or motivation required to explore the Islamic scripture in its entirety. In fact, topical selections are even more essential for non-Muslims who, while curious to obtain a first hand acquaintance with its contents, often find the arrangement and style of the Qur'an to be daunting and lack the patience to navigate a text which loses in translation much of the linguistic excellence and audible beauty and resonance of the Arabic original.

The present selection does not claim to be exhaustive, as the range of topics dealt with in the Qur'an, or those which may be of significant or even urgent relevance for certain readers, is much greater than can be covered in a book of modest length and scope as the present one. Nor is it meant as a substitute for a fuller study of the Qur'an, although it can serve as a first guide for those intending to embark on the rewarding journey through the territory of the Qur'an.

PART ONE

Worldview and Doctrine

Chapter 1

Reason and Revelation

Rationality as the Basis of Belief

Islam is a religion based on rationality and pursuit of true knowledge. The Holy Qur'an is unique among the sacred scriptures of world religions in its great emphasis on the guiding role of reason and the authority of knowledge. The Qur'an teaches that one should seek to understand the world and its Creator with knowledge and insight and base one's fundamental beliefs on conscious and conscientious reasoning.

In the verses chosen under this head, the Qur'an calls upon everyone to meditate on the creation of the heavens and the earth, and emphasizes that careful consideration of the natural phenomena sharpens one's insight and leads to knowledge. These verses specifically emphasize insight.

☐   Have they not contemplated the dominions of the heavens and the earth and whatever things God has created, and that maybe their time has already drawn near? So what discourse will they believe after this?! (7:185)

☐   In the earth are signs for those who have conviction, and in your souls as well. Will you not then perceive? (51:20-21)

☐   Do they not see that We carry water to the parched earth and with it We bring forth crops from which they themselves and their cattle eat? Will they not then see? (32:27)

☐ Those who remember God standing, sitting, and lying on their sides, and reflect on the creation of the heavens and the earth and say, 'Our Lord, You have not created this in vain! Immaculate are You! Save us from the punishment of the Fire. (3:191)

☐ God alternates the night and the day. There is indeed a lesson in that for those who have insight. (24:44)

Revelation as the Source of Guidance

Thought and inquiry can open the way for a genuine search to find answers to life's big questions: Who are we human beings? Are we different from other animals in merely possessing large brains, unmatched mental abilities, or do we have a special mission in our lives? What is the meaning of life? Why are we here? What happens when we die? Do we have a Creator to whom we are responsible for our deeds? But these question cannot be answered by empirical methods.

These and similar questions can be answered convincingly only with the help of a knowledge originating from a source beyond the realms of empirical knowledge. That transcendent source can be no other than the very Source of life and being: God, the Creator and the Guide. Divine guidance reaches us through revelations given to certain individuals who have claimed to be God's envoys. According to the Qur'an, when Adam and Eve were expelled from the Garden, God promised them the means of sustenance in their new terrestrial habitat along with the promise of guidance. God said to them, 'On the earth shall be your abode and sustenance for a time,' and He told them, 'Should any guidance come to you from Me, those who follow My guidance shall have no fear, nor shall they grieve.' (2:39)

In the same way that God has promised to provide for the material needs of humans, He has also taken upon Himself the task of providing them with guidance in order to be enable them to complete the terms of their earthly existence with success.

The books of the Hebrew Bible and the Gospels[1] are the scriptures that derive from the teachings of past prophets of the Abrahamic tradition. However, the undeniable role of human compilers, editors, redactors and translators in the formation of these books, which extended over a period of more than six hundred years (from the time of the destruction of the First Temple and the Exile to the dawn of the second Christian century, when the last of the Gospels came to be written), as suggested by Biblical scholarship, makes them less than a certain source of revealed knowledge. This is demonstrated by the vast variance among Jewish and Christian faithful about basic eschatological beliefs about the end times, resurrection of the dead, judgement and afterlife. The Qur'an, while it confirms the general role of the Torah and the Gospel as earlier witnesses of the tradition of guidance, affirms the veracity of its own contents and its own role as criterion for evaluating the statements of past scriptures and as a cue to their lacunae.

---

[1] The four gospels are centered on the figure of Jesus and believed to describe his words and deeds. As such, they have priority over other books of the NT, including Acts of the Apostles and epistles of Paul, Peter, James and John, though are also regarded as part of the canon by the Christians.

- With God rests guidance to the straight path, and some of the paths are devious, and had He wished He would have guided you all. (16:9)

- Whoever takes recourse in God is certainly guided to a straight path. (3:101)

- Say, 'Is there anyone among your partners (that is, idols and fake deities) who may guide to the truth?' Say, 'God guides to the truth. Is He who guides to the truth worthier to be followed, or he who is not guided unless he is shown the way? What is the matter with you? How do you judge?' (10:35)

- We sent down Torah containing guidance and light. The prophets, who had submitted, judged by it for the Jews, and so did the rabbis and the scribes, as they were charged to preserve the Book of God and were witnesses to it. We followed them with Jesus son of Mary to confirm that which was before him of Torah, and We gave him the Gospel containing guidance and light, confirming what was before it of Torah, and as guidance and advice for the Godwary. (5:44-46)

- God has sent down to you the Book with the truth, confirming what was revealed before it, and He had sent down the Torah and the Gospel before as guidance for mankind, and He has sent down the Criterion. Indeed, there is a severe punishment for those who deny the signs of God, and God is all-mighty, avenger. (3:3-4)

- This is the Book, there is no doubt in it, a guidance to the Godwary. (2:2)

- O People of the Book! Certainly Our Apostle has come to you, clarifying for you much of what you used to hide of the Book, and excusing many an offense of yours. Certainly, there has come to you a light from God and a manifest Book. With it God guides those who pursue His pleasure to the ways of peace, and brings them out from darkness into light by His will, and guides them to a straight path. (5:15)

☐ This Qur'an is not a fabricated discourse; rather, it is a confirmation of what was revealed before it, and an elaboration of all things, and guidance and mercy for people who have faith. (12:111)

☐ This Qur'an indeed guides to what is most upright, and gives the good news to the faithful who do righteous deeds that there is a great reward for them. (17:8-9)

☐ We have sent down the Book to you as a clarification of all things and as guidance, mercy and good news for those who submit to God. (16:89)

☐ O mankind! There has certainly come to you an advice from your Lord, and cure for what is in the breasts, and guidance and mercy for the faithful. (10:57)

☐ Say, 'O mankind! The truth has already come to you from your Lord. Whoever is guided, is guided only for the good of his own soul, and whoever goes astray, goes astray only to its detriment, and it is not my business to watch over you.' (10:108)

☐ Say, 'I only follow what is revealed to me from my Lord; these are insights from your Lord, and guidance and mercy for people who have faith.' (7:203)

☐ This (Qur'an) is an explanation for mankind, and a guidance and advice for the Godwary. (3:138)

☐ Say, 'It is God's guidance which is true guidance, and we have been commanded to submit to the Lord of all the nations, (6:71)

☐ Certainly, We have brought them a Book, which We have elaborated with knowledge, as guidance and mercy for a people who have faith. (7:52)

☐ Among the people are those who dispute concerning

God without knowledge or guidance, or an enlightening scripture, turning aside disdainfully to lead others astray from the way of God. For such there is disgrace in this world, and on the Day of Resurrection We will make him taste the punishment of the burning: 'That is because of what your hands have sent ahead, and because God is not tyrannical to the servants.' (22:8)

☐ On that day We will resurrect from every nation a group of those who denied Our signs, and they will be held in check. When they come, He will say, 'Did you deny My signs without comprehending them in knowledge? (27:8)

☐ Say, 'Insights have already come to you from your Lord. So whoever sees, it is to the benefit of his own soul, and whoever remains blind, it is to its detriment, and I am not a keeper over you.' (6:104)

☐ Say, 'This is my way. I summon to God with insight—I and he who follows me. Immaculate is God, and I am not one of the polytheists.' (12:108)

Chapter 2

Knowing God

The Signs of God's Existence

Monotheism is one of the fundamental principles of Islam and its theology, which expects that every human being should know his/her God and believe in Him. One way to know God is to reflect about the signs of God in the universe. Although an innate consciousness of God has been placed in human nature, it is sometimes clouded by external factors that shape beliefs. Therefore, thought and meditation about the signs of God's existence and His Work is a reliable process that leads the human being to His knowledge.

In the following select verses, a series of diverse phenomena in the natural world are presented as signs of the God's existence as well as His power and knowledge. Everyone who looks at them carefully and contemplates their marvellous order and harmony is guided to their creator.

☐ Blessed is He in whose hands is all sovereignty and He has power over all things. He, who created death and life that He may test you [to see] which of you is best in conduct. And He is the All-mighty, the All-forgiving. He created seven heavens in layers. You do not see any discordance in the creation of the

All-beneficent. Look again! Do you see any flaw? Look again once more. Your look will return to you, humbled and weary. (67:1-4)

☐ The apostles said (to their doubting audience), 'Is there any doubt about God, the originator of the heavens and the earth?! He calls you to forgive you a part of your sins, and grants you respite until a specified time.'
They replied, 'You are nothing but humans like us who desire to bar us from what our fathers used to worship. So bring us a clear authority.' (14:10)

☐ It is He who made the sun a radiance and the moon a light, and ordained its phases that you might know the number of years and the calculation of time. God did not create all that except with consummate wisdom. He elaborates the signs for a people who have knowledge. (10:05)

☐ It is He who has spread out the earth and set in it firm mountains and streams, and of every fruit He has made in it two kinds. He draws the night's cover over the day. There are indeed signs in that for people who reflect. (13:03)

☐ Among His signs is the creation of the heavens and the earth, and the difference of your languages and colours. There are indeed signs in that for those who know. (30:22)

☐ Among His signs is the creation of the heavens and the earth and whatever creatures He has scattered in them, and He is able to gather them whenever He wishes. (42:29)

☐ Among His signs is that you see the earth desolate; but when We send down water upon it, it stirs and swells. Indeed, He who revives it will also revive the dead. Indeed, He has power over all things. (41:39)

☐ Have they not regarded the birds disposed in the air of the sky: no one sustains them except God. There are indeed signs in that for people who have faith. (16:79)

☐ Have they not regarded the earth, how many of every splendid kind of vegetation We have caused to grow in it? There is indeed a sign in that; but most of them do not have faith. (26:7-8)

☐ Do they not see that We carry water to the parched earth and with it We bring forth crops from which they themselves and their cattle eat? Will they not then see? (32:27)

☐ Your Lord is indeed God, who created the heavens and the earth in six days, and then settled on the Throne. He draws the night's cover over the day, which pursues it swiftly, and He created the sun, the moon, and the stars, all of them disposed by His command. Lo! All creation and command belong to Him. Blessed is God, the Lord of all the nations. (7:54)

☐ It is God who raised the heavens without any pillars that you see, and then presided over the Throne. He disposed the sun and the moon, each moving for a specified term. He directs the command, and elaborates the signs that you may be certain of encountering your Lord. (13:2)

☐ It is God who sends the winds. Then they generate a cloud, then He spreads it as He wishes in the sky, and forms it into fragments, whereat you see the rain issuing from its midst. Then, when He strikes with it whomever of His servants that He wishes, behold, they rejoice; (30:48)

☐ It is God who made for you the earth an abode and the sky a canopy. He formed you and perfected your forms, and provided you with all the good things. That is God, your Lord! Blessed is God, Lord of all the nations! (40:64)

The Oneness of God

In addition to believing in the existence of God, humans

must also believe in His oneness and non-existence of anyone who should be His partner or peer. One should recognize God as the sole sovereign of the universe and the sole object of worship and veneration. God-sent prophets, especially the great Prophet of Islam, have focused more on this subject; since the existence of a supreme deity is accepted by almost all polytheists, but most of their deviations arise from a belief in other deities, whom they consider to be God's partners or independent actors in administering the affairs of the physical as well as the human world.

In polytheistic mythologies, like those of the Babylonians, Egyptians, Greeks, Romans, Arabs, and other ancient peoples, even the supreme deity was conceived as having a human form and as possessing spouses and offspring.

Even among Abrahamic faiths, which are considered to be staunchly monotheist, there have been tendencies to depict God in physical and anthropomorphic terms, as is apparent from several passages of the Hebrew Bible. These tendencies go further in Christianity, which emerged as an offshoot of the Mosaic tradition, which left no apparent room for a separate deity. When Jesus, a prophet according to Islam, came to be worshipped as God's uncreated Son by Hellenic Christians, he was conflated with God the Father along with the Holy Spirit—an angel according to Islamic belief—to form the concept of a triune deity.

The Qur'an rejects all pagan mythologies as well as the anthropomorphic formulations of Christian theology. In verses chosen for this topic, there are clear arguments for asserting the oneness of God and rejecting of all partners, conflated persons, collaborators and independent agents.

☐   Nothing is like Him and He is the All-hearing, the All-seeing. (42:11)

☐   Say, 'He is God, the One. God is the All-embracing. He neither begat, nor was begotten, nor has He any equal.' (112:1-4)

☐   Christ would never disdain being a servant of God, nor would the angels brought near [to Him]. And whoever disdains His worship and is arrogant, He will gather them all toward Him. (4:172)

☐   And when God will say (on the Day of Judgement), 'O Jesus son of Mary! Was it you who said to the people, "Take me and my mother for gods besides God"?' He will reply, 'Immaculate are You! It does not behoove me to say what I have no right to. Had I said it, You would certainly have known it: You know whatever is in my self, and I do not know what is in Your Self. Indeed, You know best all that is Unseen. I did not say to them [anything] except what You had commanded me [to say]: "Worship God, my Lord and your Lord." And I was a witness to them so long as I was among them. But when You had taken me away, You Yourself were watchful over them, and You are witness to all things. If You punish them, they are indeed Your servants; but if You forgive them, You are indeed the All-mighty, the All-wise.' (5:116-118)

☐   They say, 'The All-beneficent has offspring.' Immaculate is He! Indeed, they are His honoured servants. (22:26)

☐   They say, 'The All-beneficent has offspring!' You have certainly advanced something hideous! The heavens are about to be rent apart at it, the earth to split open, and the mountains to collapse into bits, that they should ascribe offspring to the All-beneficent! It does not behoove the All-beneficent to have offspring. There is none in the heavens and the earth but he comes to the All-beneficent as a servant. (19:88-93)

☐ Had there been any gods in the heaven and the earth other than God, they would surely have fallen apart. Clear is God, the Lord of the Throne, of what they allege concerning Him.

He is not questioned concerning what He does, but they are questioned. (21:22-24)

☐ Blessed is He who sent down the Criterion to His servant that he may be a warner to all the nations. He, to whom belongs the sovereignty of the heavens and the earth, and who did not take up any offspring, nor has He any partner in sovereignty, and He created everything and determined it in a precise measure. (25:1-2)

☐ Whoever invokes another god besides God of which he has no proof, his reckoning will indeed rest with his Lord. The faithless will indeed not prosper. (23:117)

☐ Say, 'Do you worship, besides God, what has no power to bring you any benefit or harm, while God—He is the All-hearing, the All-knowing?!' (5:76)

☐ Indeed, those whom you invoke besides God are creatures like you. So invoke them: they should answer you, if you are truthful. (7:194)

☐ The parable of those who take protectors instead of God is that of the spider that makes a home, and indeed the frailest of homes is the home of a spider, had they known! (29:41)

☐ They are certainly faithless who say, 'God is the third [person] of a trinity,' while there is no god except the One God. If they do not desist from what they say, there shall befall the faithless among them a painful punishment. Will they not repent to God and plead to Him for forgiveness? Yet God is all-forgiving, all-merciful.

The Christ, son of Mary, is but an apostle. Certainly [other] apostles have passed before him, and his mother was a truthful one. Both of them would eat food. Look how We clarify the signs for them, and yet, look, how they go astray!

Say, 'Do you worship, besides God, what has no power to bring you any benefit or harm, while God—He is the All-hearing, the All-knowing?!'

Say, 'O People of the Book! Do not unduly exceed the bounds in your religion and do not follow the myths of a people who went astray in the past and led many astray, and themselves strayed from the right path.' (5:73-77)

☐ That is God, your Lord, there is no god except Him, the creator of all things; so worship Him. He watches over all things. (6:102)

☐ And do not invoke another god besides God; there is no god except Him. Everything is to perish except His Face. All judgement belongs to Him and to Him you will be brought back. (28:88)

God's Names and Attributes

The Holy Qur'an has mentioned various names and attributes of God, each of which has its own specific field of meaning, and they are often called 'the best' or 'the most beautiful names' *(al-asmā al-husnā)*. These depict the all-encompassing and infinite greatness of God and His exclusive role in creation and fashioning of all creatures and sustaining their existence.

☐ He is God—there is no god except Him—the Sovereign, the All-holy, the All-benign, the Securer, the All-conserver, the All-mighty, the All-compeller and the All-magnanimous. Clear is God of any partners that they may ascribe to Him! He is God, the Creator, the Maker and the Former. To Him belong the Best Names. Whatever there is in the heavens and the earth glorifies Him and He is the All-mighty, the All-wise. (59:23-24)

☐ God knows what every female carries in her womb, and what the wombs reduce and what they increase, and everything is by precise measure with Him, the Knower of the sensible and the Unseen, the All-great, the All-sublime. (13:8-9)

☐ Nothing is indeed hidden from God in the earth or in the sky. It is He who forms you in the wombs of your mothers however He wishes. There is no god except Him, the All-mighty, the All-wise. (3:5-6)

☐ Do they not know that God knows their secret thoughts and hears their secret talks and that God is knower of all that is Unseen? (9:78)

God, the All-Beneficent and the All-Merciful

The verse 'In the Name of God, the All-Beneficent and the All-Merciful' occurs more than 110 times in the Qur'an and mostly at the head of surahs. Of all Divine Names, the ones which occur most often in the Qur'an are *ar-Rahmān* and *ar-Rahīm*, often translated as 'the All-Beneficent' and 'the All Merciful' respectively. Both derive from the same root, *rahmah* (mercy). In the sources, *ar-Rahmān* is interpreted to signify God's all-embracing mercy, which envelopes all existents and extends to all creatures and persons, the good and the bad, the obedient and the disobedient, those who submit to God and those who are rebellious. *Ar-Rahīm* signifies His special mercy, enjoyed by those who have faith in Him and follow His guidance. These points are further elaborated in the following verses.

☐ 'I visit My punishment on whomever I wish, but My mercy embraces all things.' (7:156)

☐ 'To whom belongs whatever there is in the heavens and the earth?' Say, 'To God. He has made mercy binding for

Himself. He will surely gather you on the Day of Resurrection, in which there is no doubt. (6:12)

When those who have faith in Our signs come to you, say, 'Peace to you! Your Lord has made mercy incumbent upon Himself: whoever of you commits an evil deed out of ignorance and then repents after that and reforms, then He is indeed all-forgiving, all-merciful.'(6:54)

- God singles out for His mercy whomever He wishes, and God is dispenser of a mighty grace. (2:105)

- Obey God and the Apostle so that you may be granted His mercy. (3:132)

- As for those who have faith in God and hold fast to Him, He will admit them to His mercy and grace, and He will guide them on a straight path to Him. (4:175)

- 'Your Lord is dispenser of an all-embracing mercy, but His punishment will not be averted from the guilty lot.' (6:147)

- Do not cause corruption on the earth after its restoration, and supplicate Him with fear and hope: indeed God's mercy is close to the virtuous. (7:56)

- Moses said, 'My Lord, forgive me and my brother and admit us into Your mercy, for You are the most merciful of the merciful. (7:157)

- Say, 'In God's grace and His mercy—let them rejoice in that! It is better than what they amass.' (10:58)

- As for those who have faith and do righteous deeds, their Lord will admit them into His mercy. That is a manifest triumph! (5:30)

- Had your Lord wished, He would have made mankind one community; but they continue to differ, except those on whom your Lord has mercy—and that is why He created them. (11:118)

☐ We did not send down the Book to you except for the purpose that you may clarify for them what they differ about, and as guidance and mercy for people who have faith. (16:64)

☐ (A prayer of Solomon): 'My Lord! Inspire me to give thanks for Your blessing with which You have blessed me and my parents, and that I may do righteous deeds which please You, and admit me, by Your mercy, among Your righteous servants.' (27:19)

☐ So observe the effects of God's mercy: how He revives the earth after its death! He is indeed the reviver of the dead and He has power over all things. (30:50)

☐ The Day of Judgement is indeed the tryst for them all, the day when a friend will not avail a friend in any way, nor will they be helped, except for him on whom God has mercy. Indeed, He is the All-mighty, the All-merciful. (43:40-42)

The Forgiver of Sins

One of God's names in the Qur'an is 'the Forgiver.' He forgives sin and disobedience and accepts the repentance of His servants (40:3). Islam does not recognize the notion of original sin, a condition of unmitigated, hereditary sinfulness and congenital guilt inherited by all born of Adam and eve.

According to the Qur'an, Adam and Eve—unlike Satan, who rebelled against God and persisted in his rebellion—repented soon after their act of disobedience and God accepted their repentance (2:37; 20:122). Moreover, although individuals may suffer and be hurt by others' sins, no individual can be held responsible for the sins of another, as this is contrary to justice. Guilt cannot be hereditary. To forgive the sins of creatures is a Divine prerogative and is not contrary to justice.

Further, although the Qur'an posits the notion of intercession, which can happen only by God's permission (4:64, 2:255), no one can expiate for another's sins. Hence the Christian doctrine of Atonement with all its variants is foreign to the Qur'an, inasmuch as it is stranger to the Hebrew Bible.

In the following verses, God promises forgiveness for all who turn penitently to Him and submit to Him while there is still time. Some of the great angels are also portrayed as seeking forgiveness and deliverance for the faithful and the repentant.

☐ O My servants who have committed excesses against their own souls, do not despair of the mercy of God. God will indeed forgive all sins. Indeed, He is the All-forgiving, the All-merciful. Turn penitently to Him and submit to Him before the punishment overtakes you, whereupon you will not be helped. And follow the best of what has been sent down to you from your Lord, before the punishment overtakes you suddenly while you are unaware.' (39:53-55)

☐ Had they, when they had wronged themselves, come to you (O Muhammad) and pleaded to God for forgiveness, and the Apostle had pleaded forgiveness for them, they would have surely found God clement and merciful. (4:64)

☐ Those (angels) who bear the Throne and those who are around it celebrate the praise of their Lord and have faith in Him, and they plead forgiveness for the faithful: 'Our Lord! You embrace all things in Your mercy and knowledge. So forgive those who repent and follow Your way and save them from the punishment of hell. Our Lord! Admit them into the Gardens of Eden, which You have promised them, along with whoever is righteous among their forebears, their spouses and their descendants. Indeed, You are the All-mighty, the All-wise. Save them from the ills of the Day of Resurrection, and whomever You save from the ills that day, You will have had mercy upon him, and that is a mighty triumph.' (40:7-9)

CHAPTER 3

The Human Being in the Qur'an

Man, God's Viceroy on Earth

The Qur'anic story of Adam's creation and fall is emblematic of how the human being is regarded is the Islamic worldview. God declares to the angels His intention to install a representative on the earth. The angels voice their doubts about the wisdom of such an undertaking. Ultimately, when Adam is created from clay and after a phase of Divine instruction proves that his higher faculties lie beyond the ken of the angels, they are ordered to bow down before him in veneration. Satan, who is really a jinn and not an angel, refuses to acknowledge Adam's superiority and is cast away from Divine presence. Adam and Eve are deceived by their enemy into eating from the forbidden tree and are expelled from their heavenly grace to cope with the hardships of an earthly mortal existence and struggle against the unending ruses and seductions of an invisible unrelenting enemy.

▢   When your Lord said to the angels, 'I am indeed going to set a viceroy on the earth,' they said, 'Will You set in it someone who will cause corruption in it and shed blood, while we celebrate Your praise and proclaim Your sanctity?' He said, 'Indeed, I know what you do not know.'

God taught Adam the Names, all of them; then He presented them to the angels and said, 'Tell me the names of these, if you are truthful.' They said, 'Immaculate are You! We have no knowledge except what You have taught us. Indeed, You are the All-knowing, the All-wise.'

God said, 'O Adam, inform them of their names,' and when he had informed them of their names, He said, 'Did I not tell you that I know the Unseen of the heavens and the earth, and that I know whatever you disclose and whatever you conceal?'

And when God said to the angels, 'Prostrate before Adam,' they prostrated, but not Iblis: he refused and acted arrogantly, and he was one of the faithless.

We said, 'O Adam, dwell with your mate in paradise, and eat thereof freely whencesoever you wish, but do not approach this tree, lest you should be among the wrongdoers.' Then Satan caused them to stumble from it, and he dislodged them from what [state] they were in; and We said, 'Get down, being enemies of one another! On the earth shall be your abode and sustenance for a time.'

Then Adam received certain words from his Lord, and He turned to him clemently. Indeed, He is the All-clement, the All-merciful.

God said, 'Get down from it, all together! Yet, should any guidance come to you from Me, those who follow My guidance shall have no fear, nor shall they grieve. But those who are faithless and deny Our signs, they shall be the inmates of the Fire and they shall remain in it [forever].

Despite his vulnerabilities and weakness, the human being has a higher vocation because of his sublime abilities, talents and gifts. Therefore, the Holy Qur'an introduces him as the flower of creation (at least, in this part of our immense universe, and in this brief era sandwiched between enormously long eons and stretches of time[1]), for whose benefit everything has been prepared, from sun, moon and the stars to mountains and seas. Everything in the heavens and the earth has been disposed for his benefit.

☐ Do you not see that God has disposed for you whatever there is in the heavens and whatever there is in the earth, and He has showered upon you His blessings, the outward and the inward? Yet among the people are those who dispute concerning God without any knowledge or guidance or an illuminating scripture. (31:20)

☐ He disposed the night and the day for you, and the sun, the moon and the stars are disposed by His command. There are indeed signs in that for people who exercise their reason.

And He disposed for your benefit whatever He has created for you in the earth of diverse hues—there is indeed a sign in that for people who take admonition.

It is He who disposed the sea for your benefit that you may eat from it fresh meat, and obtain from it ornaments which you wear, and you see the ships ploughing through it, so that you may seek of His bounty and that you may give thanks.

---

[1] That is, keeping in view not only the findings of modern astronomy and palaeontology, but also certain traditions narrated from the Shi'i Imams, according to which 'a million Adams' (*alfa alfin ādam*) and 'a million races' (*alfa alfin 'ālam*) of intelligent beings have preceded the emergence of 'our Adam' and the human race. They also state that seven anthropoid species (*sab'ata 'ālamīn*) have preceded the emergence of present humankind and children of Adam on this earth itself. Other traditions state that after this earth has been laid waste, God's creation of intelligent species and nations (*awālim*) will go on 'in other earths' and 'under other heavens' after our Day of Judgement and after our righteous humans have been admitted into paradise and our guilty have entered hell.

See *al-Khisal*, vol. 2, 652, hadith no. 54, whence *Bihar al-anwar*, vol. 8, 374-375, hadith no. 2 & *al-Tawhid*, 277, hadith no. 2, whence in *Bihar al-anwar*, vol. 54, 321, hadith no. 3. *Al-Khisal*, vol. 2, 358-9, hadith 49, whence *Bihar al-anwar*, vol. 8, 374, hadith no. 1.

He cast firm mountains in the earth lest it should shake with you, and made streams and ways so that you may be guided —and the landmarks as well—and by the stars they are guided. (16:12-16)

☐ It is God who created the heavens and the earth, and He sends down water from the sky and brings forth with it crops for your sustenance.

And He disposed the ships for your benefit, so that they may sail at sea by His command, and He disposed the rivers for you. He disposed the sun and the moon for you, constant in their courses, and He disposed the night and the day. (14:32-33)

Human Nature

One of the characteristics of man is his intellect and spirit that raises his higher than the animals and the plants, which is also called human nature.

In human nature there are tendencies towards spirituality and moral values, the most important of which is his urge for the knowledge of the Divine. On the basis of this innate inclination, the human being is bound by a covenant not to worship anyone other than God.

☐ So set your heart as a person of pure faith on this religion, the original nature endowed by God according to which He originated mankind. There is no altering God's creation; that is the upright religion, but most people do not know. (30:30)

☐ When your Lord took from the Children of Adam, their seed from their loins, and made them bear witness over themselves, He said to them, 'Am I not your Lord?' They said, 'Yes indeed! We bear witness.' This, lest you should say on the Day of Resurrection, 'We were indeed unaware of this,' or lest you should say, 'Our fathers ascribed partners to God before us and we were descendants after them. Will You then destroy us because of what the falsifiers did?' (7:172-173)

☐ By the soul and Him who fashioned it, and inspired it with discernment between virtues and vices: one who purifies it is felicitous and one who betrays it fails. (91:7-10)

☐ 'Did I not exhort you, O children of Adam, saying, "Do not worship Satan. He is indeed your manifest enemy. Worship Me. That is a straight path"? (36:60-61)

Human dignity

According to the Qur'an, the human being has a high status among the creatures because of his many gifts and innate inclination toward God. He had a special creation and was endowed with unprecedented potentialities that made him worthy of the prostration of the angels. The essential being of Adam's children is imbued with an inherent dignity, which can be further enhanced with acquired merit.

☐ Certainly We have honoured the Children of Adam and carried them over land and sea, and provided them with all the good things, and preferred them with a complete preference over many of those We have created. (17:70)

☐ 'O soul at peace! Return to your Lord, pleased with Him and pleasing to Him! Then enter among My servants and enter My paradise!' (89:27-30)

☐ Of His signs is that He created for you mates from your own selves that you may take comfort in them, and He ordained affection and mercy between you. There are indeed signs in that for a people who reflect. (30:21)

Man on the Path of Evolution

Man has always been on an evolutionary course because of his intellect, his talents and his tools. He has a boundless capacity to learn and God taught him what he did not know. Man was entrusted with a trust and bore what the heavens and the earth and the mountains could not carry. This is the dynamic source of his spiritual and intellectual evolution.

☐ Has there been a period of time for man when he was not anything worthy of mention? We indeed created man from the drop of a mixed fluid so that We may put him to test, so We endowed him with hearing and sight. We have indeed guided him to the way, be he grateful or ungrateful. (76:1-3)

☐ The All-beneficent has taught the Qur'an. He created man, and taught him articulate speech. (55:1-4)

☐ God has brought you forth from the bellies of your mothers while you did not know anything. He invested you with hearing, sight, and the hearts, so that you may give thanks. (16:78)

☐ That is the Knower of the sensible and the Unseen, the All-mighty, the All-merciful, who perfected everything that He created and commenced man's creation from clay. (32:6-9)

☐ Then He made his progeny from an extract of a base fluid. Then He proportioned him and breathed into him of His Spirit, and invested you with your hearing, sight, and hearts. Little do you thank.
Say, 'Everyone acts according to his character. Your Lord knows best who is better guided with regard to the way.' (17:84)

☐ Whoever strives, strives only for his own sake. God has indeed no need of the creatures. As for those who have faith and do righteous deeds, e will absolve them of their misdeeds and We will surely reward them by the best of what they used to do. (29:6-7)

☐ By the soul and Him who fashioned it, and inspired it with discernment between its virtues and vices: one who purifies it is felicitous and one who betrays it fails. (91:7-10)

☐ Indeed, We presented the Trust to the heavens and the earth and the mountains, but they refused to undertake it and were apprehensive of it; but man undertook it. He is indeed most ignorant and unjust. (33:72)

☐ Even as We sent to you an Apostle from among yourselves, who recites to you Our signs and purifies you, and teaches you the Book and wisdom, and teaches you what you did not know. (2:151)

☐ Read in the Name of your Lord who created; created man from a clinging mass.
Read, and your Lord is the most generous, who taught by the pen, taught man what he did not know. (96:1-5)

☐ And to Thamūd We sent Sālih, their kinsman. He said, 'O my people! Worship God. You have no other god besides Him. He brought you forth from the earth and made it your habitation. So plead with Him for forgiveness, then turn to Him penitently. My Lord is indeed nearmost and responsive.' (11:61)

☐ We certainly created man in the best of forms; then We relegated him to the lowest of the low, except those who have faith and do righteous deeds. There will be an everlasting reward for them. (95:4-6)

☐ O you who have faith! When you are told, 'Make room,' in sittings, then do make room; God will make room for you. And when you are told, 'Rise up!' Do rise up. God will raise in rank those of you who have faith and those who have been given knowledge, and God is well aware of what you do. (58:11)

☐ For everyone there are ranks in accordance with what they have done, and your Lord is not oblivious of what they do. (6:132)

☐ Indeed, those who say, 'Our Lord is God!' and then remain steadfast, the angels descend upon them, saying, 'Do not fear, nor be grieved! Receive the good news of the paradise which you have been promised. (41:30)

☐ Soon We will show them Our signs in the horizons and in their own souls until it becomes clear to them that He is the Real. Is it not sufficient that your Lord is witness to all things? (41:53)

Human Life a Test and Trial

Every human being has a long way to go to attain the position worthy of her/him, including that she/he must be put to the test throughout the course of her/his life. The tests faced by individuals vary depending on their situation. Sometimes people are tested with hardships and sometimes with blessings. What comes as a test is to give the person a chance to get closer to God and to rise to a higher level. Of course, some persons may fail the test and do something that may cause them to go down.

These verses describe various kinds of divine tests and their possible results.

☐ Do the people suppose that they will be let off because they say, 'We have faith,' and they will not be tested? Certainly We tested those who were before them. So God shall surely ascertain those who are truthful and He shall surely ascertain the liars. (29:2-3)

☐   We will surely test you with a measure of fear and hunger and a loss of wealth, lives, and fruits; and give good news to the patient—those who, when an affliction visits them, say, 'Indeed, we belong to God and to Him do we indeed return.' It is they who receive the blessings of their Lord and His mercy, and it is they who are the rightly guided. (2:155-157)

☐   We have sent down to you the Book with the truth, confirming what went before it of the scripture and as a guardian over it. So judge between them by what God has sent down, and do not follow their base desires contrary to the truth that has come to you.
For each community among you We had appointed a code of law and a path, and had God wished He would have made you one community, but His purposes required that He should test you with respect to what He has given you.
So take the lead in all good works. To God shall be the return of you all, whereat He will inform you concerning that about which you used to differ. (5:48)

☐   Blessed is He in whose hands is all sovereignty and He has power over all things. He, who created death and life that He may test you to see which of you is best in conduct. And He is the All-mighty, the All-forgiving. (67:1-2)

☐   We indeed created man from the drop of a mixed fluid so that We may put him to test, so We endowed him with hearing and sight. We have indeed guided him to the way, be he grateful or ungrateful. (76:2-3)

☐   It is He who has made you successors on the earth, and raised some of you in rank above others so that He may test you with respect to what He has given you. Your Lord is indeed swift in retribution, and He is indeed all-forgiving, all-merciful. (6:165)

☐   Indeed, We have made whatever is on the earth an

adornment for it that We may test them to see which of them is best in conduct. (18:7)

☐ Every soul shall taste death, and We will test you with good and ill by way of test, and to Us you will be brought back. (21:35)

☐ We dispersed them (i.e., the Israelites) throughout communities around the earth: some of them were righteous, and some of them otherwise, and We tested them with good and bad times so that they may come back. (7:168)

☐ We have made you a means of test for one another, to see if you will be patient and steadfast, and your Lord is all-seeing. (25:20)

Divine Traditions in History

From the Qur'an's point of view, the driving force behind the movement of history and the rise and fall of societies are the traditions of God in human society. The traditions of God are the immutable laws of history that are like natural laws and they never change.

In the verses we have chosen some of these traditions are mentioned and people are invited to think about them and to draw lesson from what has gone on in past societies

☐ Indeed, God does not change a people's lot, unless they change what is in their souls. And when God wishes to visit ill on a people, there is nothing that can avert it, and they have no protector besides Him. (13:11)

☐ So do they await anything except the precedent of the ancients? Yet you will never find any change in God's precedent, and you will never find any revision in God's precedent.

Have they not travelled through the land so that they may observe how was the fate of those who were before them? They were more powerful than them, and God is not to be frustrated by anything in the heavens or on the earth. He is indeed all-knowing, all-powerful. (35:43-44)

☐ If wounds afflict you, like wounds have already afflicted those people; and We make such vicissitudes rotate among mankind, so that God may ascertain those who have faith, and that He may take martyrs from among you, and God does not like the wrongdoers. And so that God may purge the hearts of those who have faith and that He may wipe out the faithless. (3:140-141)

☐ And We desired to show favour to those who were oppressed in the land, and to make them imams and to make them the heirs, (28:5)

☐ Have they not regarded how many a generation We have destroyed before them whom We had granted power in the land in respects that We did not grant you, and We sent abundant rains for them from the sky and made streams run for them? Then We destroyed them for their sins, and brought forth another generation after them. (6:6)

☐ Have they not travelled through the land to observe how was the fate of those who were before them? God destroyed them and a similar fate awaits these faithless. That is because God is the Master of the faithful, and because the faithless have no master. (47:10-11)

☐ Apostles were certainly denied before you, yet they patiently bore being denied and tormented until Our help came to them.
Nothing can change the words of God, and there have certainly come to you some of the accounts of the apostles. (6:34)

☐ If God helps you, no one can overcome you, but if He forsakes you, who will help you after Him? So in God alone let all the faithful put their trust. (3:160)

☐ So when they forgot what they had been reminded of, We delivered those who forbade evil conduct and seized the wrongdoers with a terrible punishment because of the transgressions they used to commit. (7:165)

☐ Those who were expelled from their homes unjustly, only because they said, 'God is our Lord.' Had not God repulsed the people from one another, ruin would have befallen the monasteries, churches, synagogues and mosques in which God's Name is much invoked. God will surely help those who help Him. God is indeed all-strong, all-mighty. Those who, if We granted them power in the land, will maintain the prayer, give the zakāt, bid what is right and forbid what is wrong, and with God rests the outcome of all matters. (22:40-41)

☐ We shall indeed help Our apostles and those who have faith in the life of the world and on the day when the witnesses rise up, the day when the excuses of the wrongdoers will not benefit them, the curse will lie on them, and for them will be the ills of the ultimate abode. (40:51)

☐ If the people of the towns had been faithful and God-wary, We would have opened to them blessings from the heaven and the earth. But they impugned Our apostles; so We seized them because of what they used to perpetrate. (7:96)

☐ Certainly Our decree has gone beforehand in favour of Our servants, the apostles, that they will indeed receive God's help, and indeed Our hosts will be the victors. (37:171-173)

☐ God has ordained: 'I shall surely prevail, I and My apostles.' God is indeed all-strong, all-mighty. (58:21)

Factors of the Fall of Societies

Of the Divine traditions in human society are those that relate to the collapse and destruction of societies. They pertain to the people's modes of conduct that lead to the destruction of that society. When these factors arise, the collapse of that community is inevitable, such as the institutionalization of oppression and the emergence of deep divisions in society and other factors that are mentioned in some of these verses

☐ Do those who devise evil schemes feel secure that God will not make the earth swallow them, or the punishment will not overtake them whence they are not aware? Or that He will not seize them in the midst of their bustle, whereupon they will not be able to frustrate Him? Or that He will not visit them with attrition? Your Lord is indeed most kind and merciful. (16:45-47)

☐ How many a town defied the command of its Lord and His apostles, then We called it to a severe account and punished it with a dire punishment. So it tasted the evil consequences of its conduct, and the outcome of its conduct was ruin. (65:8-9)

☐ Have you not regarded how your Lord dealt with the people of 'Ād, and Iram, the city of the pillars, the like of which was not created among cities, and the people of Thamūd, who hollowed out the rocks in the valley, and Pharaoh, the impaler —those who rebelled against God in their cities and caused much corruption in them, so your Lord poured on them lashes of punishment.
Your Lord is indeed in ambush. (89:6-14)

☐ How many a town We have smashed that had been wrongdoing, and We brought forth another people after it. (21:11)

☐ Obey God and His Apostle and do not dispute, or you will lose heart and your power will be gone. And be patient; indeed God is with the patient. (8:46)

Freedom of Choice

From the point of view of the Qur'an, people are free to choose between right and wrong, and God has not forced anyone to involuntarily follow the right path. But He has identified right and wrong and clearly stated the consequences and outcome of choosing right or wrong and invited people to the right path and it is up to man to choose which way to go..

☐ Say, 'O mankind! The truth has already come to you from your Lord. Whoever is guided, is guided only for the good of his own soul, and whoever goes astray, goes astray only to its detriment, and it is not my business to watch over you.' (10:108)

☐ Say, 'Insights have already come to you from your Lord. So whoever sees, it is to the benefit of his own soul, and whoever remains blind, it is to its detriment, and I am not a keeper over you.' (6:104)

☐ There is no compulsion in religion: rectitude has become distinct from error. So one who disavows satanic entities and has faith in God has held fast to the firmest handle for which there is no breaking; and God is all-hearing, all-knowing. (2:256)

☐ Whoever desires the tillage of the Hereafter, We will enhance for him his tillage, and whoever desires the tillage of the world, We will give it to him, but he will have no share in the Hereafter. (42:20)

☐ We indeed created man from the drop of a mixed fluid so that We may put him to test, so We endowed him with hearing and sight. We have indeed guided him to the way, be he grateful or ungrateful. (76:2-3)

☐ Does he have the knowledge of the Unseen so that he sees? Has he not been informed of what is in the scriptures of

Moses, and of Abraham, who fulfilled his summons: that no bearer shall bear another's burden, that nothing belongs to man except what he strives for, and that he will soon be shown his endeavour, then he will be requited for it with the fullest requital; (53:39-41)

☐ Is the apostles' duty anything but to communicate in clear terms? Certainly We raised an apostle in every nation to preach: 'Worship God and shun satanic entities.' Among them were some whom God guided, and among them were some who deserved to be in error. So travel through the land and observe how was the fate of the deniers. (16:35-36)

☐ The one who had knowledge of the Book said, 'I will bring it to you in the twinkling of an eye.'
So when he saw it set near him, he said, 'This is by the grace of my Lord, to test me if I will give thanks or be ungrateful. Whoever gives thanks, gives thanks only for his own sake. And whoever is ungrateful should know that my Lord is indeed all-sufficient, all-generous.' (27:40)

☐ Then We made those whom We chose from Our servants heirs to the Book. Yet some of them are those who wrong themselves, and some of them are average, and some of them are those who take the lead in all the good works by God's will. That is the great grace of God! (35:32)

☐ Indeed, We have sent down to you the Book with the truth for the deliverance of mankind. So whoever is guided is guided for his own sake, and whoever goes astray, goes astray to his own detriment, and it is not your duty to watch over them. (39:41)

☐ Whoever acts righteously, it is for the benefit of his own soul, and whoever does evil, it is to its detriment, and your Lord is not tyrannical to His servants. (41:46)

☐ This is indeed a reminder. So let anyone who wishes

take the way toward his Lord. (73:19)

☐ And say, 'This is the truth from your Lord: let anyone who wishes believe it, and let anyone who wishes disbelieve it.' We have indeed prepared for the wrongdoers a Fire whose curtains will surround them on all sides. If they cry out for help, they will be helped with a water like molten copper which will scald their faces. What an evil drink and how ill a resting place! As for those who have faith and do righteous deeds—indeed We do not waste the reward of those who are good in deeds. (18:29-30)

The Conflict Between Right and Wrong

The constant struggle between truth and falsehood throughout history has been the subject of the Qur'an and it has introduced both the truth and the falsehood as well as their adherents, so that people may consciously side with the truth and avoid falsehood.

According to these revelations, if falsehood does flourish for a few days, it will eventually disappear, and the truth will eventually prevail even if it is suppressed for a short period of time.

☐ We do not send the apostles except as bearers of good news and warners, but those who are faithless dispute fallaciously to refute thereby the truth, having taken in derision My signs and what they are warned of. (18:56)

☐ And say, 'The truth has come, and falsehood has vanished. Falsehood is indeed bound to vanish.' (17:81)

☐ He sends down water from the sky whereat the valleys are flooded to the extent of their capacity, and the flood carries along a swelling scum. A similar scum arises from what they smelt in the fire for the purpose of making ornaments or wares.

That is how God compares truth and falsehood. As for the scum, it leaves as dross, and that which profits the people stays in the earth. That is how God draws comparisons. (13:17)

☐ Do they say, 'He has fabricated a lie against God'? If so, should God wish He would set a seal on your heart, and God will efface the falsehood and confirm the truth with His words. He knows indeed well what is in the breasts. (42:24)

☐ That is because the faithless follow falsehood and those who have faith follow the truth from their Lord. That is how God draws comparisons for mankind. (47:3)

☐ It is He who has sent His Apostle with guidance and the religion of truth, that He may make it prevail over all religions, though the polytheists should be averse. (9:33)

☐ Have you not regarded that God makes the night pass into the day and makes the day pass into the night; and He has disposed the sun and the moon, each moving for a specified term, and that God is well aware of what you do? That is because God is the Reality, and whatever they invoke besides Him is nullity, and because God is the All-exalted, the All-great. (31:29-30)

☐ Those who are fought against are permitted to fight because they have been wronged, and God is indeed able to help them —those who were expelled from their homes unjustly only because they said, 'God is our Lord.' Had not God repulsed the people from one another, ruin would have befallen the monasteries, churches, synagogues and mosques in which God's Name is much invoked. God will surely help those who help Him. God is indeed all-strong, all-mighty. (22:39-40)

☐ Say, 'Indeed, my Lord hurls the truth. He is the knower of all that is Unseen.' Say, 'The truth has come and falsehood neither originates anything, nor restores anything after its demise.' (34:48-49)

☐ Say, 'Who provides for you out of the heaven and the earth? Who controls your hearing and sight, and who brings forth the living from the dead and brings forth the dead from the living, and who directs the command?' They will say, 'God.' Say, 'Will you not then be wary of Him?' That, then, is God, your true Lord. So what is there after the truth except error? Then where are you being led away? (10:31-32)

The Reign of the Righteous as the Final End of History

One of the most important Divine plans for human history is that eventually the truth will prevail over falsehood and the teaching of the prophets over the materialist schools of thought, and the rule of the righteous and the worthy will be established on earth, and the oppressed and the down-trodden in the East and the West will be the heirs and masters of the earth. This is a promise that God has made in several verses.

☐ Certainly Our decree has gone beforehand in favour of Our servants, the apostles, that they will indeed receive God's help, and indeed Our hosts will be the victors. (37:171-173)

☐ God has promised those of you who have faith and do righteous deeds that He will surely make them successors in the earth, just as He made those who were before them successors, and He will surely establish for them their religion which He has approved for them, and that He will surely change their state to security after their fear, while they worship Me, not ascribing any partners to Me. Whoever is ungrateful after that—it is they who are the transgressors. (24:55)

☐ God has ordained: 'I shall surely prevail, I and My apostles.' God is indeed all-strong, all-mighty. (58:21)

☐ We made the people who were oppressed heirs to the

east and west of the land which We had blessed, and your Lord's best word of promise was fulfilled for the Children of Israel because of their patience, and We destroyed what Pharaoh and his people had built and whatever they used to erect. (7:137)

▢   Certainly We wrote in the Psalms, after the Torah: 'My righteous servants shall indeed inherit the earth.' There is indeed in this a proclamation for a devout people. (21:105-106)

▢   O you who have faith! Should any of you desert his religion, God will soon bring a people whom He loves and who love Him, who will be humble towards the faithful, stern towards the faithless, waging jihād in the way of God, not fearing the blame of any blamer. That is God's grace which He grants to whomever He wishes, and God is all-bounteous, all-knowing. (5:54)

Chapter 4

The Role of God's Envoys

The Prophets as God's Emissaries

Another fundamental principle of Islam is prophecy. That is, to believe that God has directed certain individuals to guide humanity and lead them to the path of truth and justice, to teach them the way to live in a worthy manner and to satisfy their physical and spiritual needs along the path of sublimity and edification.

By receiving the messages of God through direct revelation, the prophets on the one hand guide human beings to attain human perfection and realize the higher values , and to lead them in the struggle for the establishment of justice and equity in society on the other.

In this section we have selected verses that describe why God had to send His messengers. They describe the significance and role of revelation and the purposes of sending the envoys.

☐ Certainly We sent Our apostles with clear proofs, and We sent down with them the Book and the Balance, so that mankind may maintain justice; and We sent down iron, in which there is great might and uses for mankind, and so that God may know those who help Him and His apostles with faith in the Unseen. God is indeed all-strong, all-mighty. (57:25)

☐ There is an apostle for every nation; so when their apostle comes, judgement is made between them with justice, and they are not wronged. (10:47)

☐ Is the apostles' duty anything but to communicate in clear terms? Certainly We raised an apostle in every nation to preach: 'Worship God and shun satanic entities.' Among them were some whom God guided, and among them were some who deserved to be in error. So travel through the land and observe how was the fate of the deniers. (16:35-36)

☐ Your Lord would not destroy the towns until He had raised an apostle in their mother city to recite Our signs to them. We would never destroy the towns except when their people were wrongdoers. (28:59)

☐ 'O community of the jinn and humans! Did there not come to you apostles from yourselves, recounting to you My signs and warning you of the encounter of this Day?' They will say, 'We do bear witness against ourselves.' The life of this world had deceived them, and they will testify against themselves that they had been faithless. (6:130)

☐ Whoever is guided is guided only for the good of his own soul, and whoever goes astray, goes astray only to its detriment. No bearer shall bear another's burden. (17:15)

☐ We do not punish any community until We have sent it an apostle. We have indeed sent you with the truth as a bearer of good news and warner, and there is not a nation but a warner has passed in it. If they impugn you, those before them have impugned likewise: their apostles brought them manifest proofs, holy writs, and illuminating scriptures. (35:24-25)

☐ We have indeed revealed to you as We revealed to Noah and the prophets after him, and as We revealed to Abraham,

Ishmael, Isaac, Jacob, and the Tribes, Jesus and Job, Jonah, Aaron and Solomon—and We gave David the Psalms (4:163)

☐ It is not possible for any human that God should speak to him,a except through revelation or from behind a veil,b or send a messenger who reveals by His permission whatever He wishes. He is indeed all-exalted, all-wise. (42:51)

☐ This was Our argument that We gave to Abraham against his people. We raise in rank whomever We wish. Your Lord is indeed all-wise, all-knowing.

And We gave him Isaac and Jacob and guided each of them. And Noah We had guided before, and from his offspring David and Solomon, Job, Joseph, Moses and Aaron—thus do We reward the virtuous— and Zechariah, John, Jesus and Elijah— each of them among the righteous— and Ishmael, Elisha, Jonah and Lot—each We preferred over all the nations— and from among their fathers, descendants and brethren—We chose them and guided them to a straight path. (6:83-87)

Attributes of the Prophets

Divine prophets and messengers sent for human guidance had attributes and qualifications, some of which are general and have been present in all the prophets, and some are specific attributes that have been in some and not others. For example, attributes such as warning and giving good news belong to all the prophets, and attributes such as an playing an epoch-making role were present in only some of them. The noble Prophet of Islam had certain attributes that none of the prophets possessed. The verses selected mention the common and specific attributes of the prophets. The attributes of the Prophet of Islam will appear in a subsequent section.

☐ We do not send the apostles except as bearers of good

news and warners. As for those who are faithful and righteous, they will have no fear, nor will they grieve. (6:48)

☐ These are the apostles, some of whom We gave an advantage over others: of them are those to whom God spoke and some of them He raised in rank, and We gave Jesus, son of Mary, manifest proofs and strengthened him with the Holy Spirit.

Had God wished, those who succeeded them would have not fought one another, after clear proofs had come to them. But they differed. There were among them those who had faith and there were those who were faithless, and had God wished, they would not have fought one another; but God does whatever He desires. (2:253)

☐ O Prophet! We have indeed sent you as a witness, as a bearer of good news and warner and as a summoner to God by His permission, and as a radiant lamp. (33:45-46)

☐ A prophet may not breach his trust, and whoever breaches his trust will bring his breaches on the Day of Resurrection; then every soul shall be recompensed fully for what it has earned, and they will not be wronged. (3:161)

☐ God certainly favoured the faithful when He raised up among them an apostle from among themselves to recite to them His signs, and to purify them and teach them the Book and wisdom, and earlier they had indeed been in manifest error. (3:164)

☐ So be patient just as the resolute among the apostles were patient, and do not seek to hasten the punishment for them. The day when they see what they are promised, it will be as though they had remained in the world just an hour of a day. This is a proclamation. Will anyone be destroyed except the transgressing lot? (46:35)

☐ —Such as deliver the messages of God and fear Him and

fear no one except God, and God suffices as reckoner. (33:39)

☐ Knower of the Unseen, He does not disclose His knowledge of the Unseen to anyone except an apostle that He approves of. Then He dispatches a sentinel before and behind him so that He may ascertain that they have delivered the messages of their Lord, and He encompasses all that is with them, and He keeps a count of all things. (72:27)

The Covenant of the Prophets

Each of the prophets who were sent by God as God's messenger actually made a covenant with God that they would spare no effort to proclaim His religion. The verses we have chosen in this section emphasize the covenants of the prophets with God, and that God has taken from them a solid and solemn covenant to communicate His religion. One of the issues the prophets have been committed to accomplish is to believe in the prophets who were to come after themselves and to inform the people of their coming and to prepare the ground for their acceptance.

☐ Recall when We took a pledge from the prophets and from you and from Noah and Abraham and Moses and Jesus son of Mary, and We took from them a solemn pledge, so that He may question the truthful concerning their truthfulness. And He has prepared for the faithless a painful punishment. (33:7-8)

☐ When God took a compact concerning the prophets, He said, 'Inasmuch as I have given you the knowledge of the Book and wisdom,b should an apostle come to you thereafter confirming what is with you, you shall believe in him and help him.' He said, 'Do you pledge and accept My covenant on this condition?' They said, 'We pledge.' Said He, 'Then be witnesses, and I, too, am among witnesses along with you.' (3:81)

Humanity of the Prophets

The prophets, with all their greatness and sacredness, were ultimately humans and had all human needs. Sometimes some of their followers would elevate their sanctity to the level of God. Sometimes they were expected to carry out superhuman deeds and to be unlike ordinary people who eat and drink and walk in the marketplaces. These verses emphasize the human aspect of the prophets, so as to counter exaggerated notions about their nature and to drive home the fact that the prophets must be members of the human race.

☐ Their apostles said to them, 'We are indeed just human beings like yourselves; but God favours whomever of His servants that He wishes. We may not bring you an authority except by God's leave, and in God alone let all the faithful put their trust. (14:11)

☐ We did not send any apostles before you but that they ate food and walked in marketplaces. We have made you a means of test for one another, to see if you will be patient and steadfast, and your Lord is all-seeing. (25:20)

☐ They say, 'Why has not an angel been sent down to him?' Were We to send down an angel, the matter would surely be decided, and then they would not be granted any respite.
Had We made him an angel, We would have surely made him a man, and We would have still confounded them just as they confound the truth now. (6:8-9)

☐ We did not send any apostle except with the language of his people, so that he might make Our messages clear to them. Then God leads astray whomever He wishes, and He guides whomsoever He wishes, and He is the All-mighty, the All-wise. (14:04)

☐ Say, 'I am just a human being like you. It has been revealed to me that your God is the One God. So worship Him single-mindedly and plead to Him for forgiveness.' And woe to the polytheists (41:6)

☐ Say, 'I am not a novelty among the apostles, nor do I know what will be done with me or with you. I just follow whatever is revealed to me, and I am just a manifest warner.' (46:9)

☐ We did not send any apostles before you except as men to whom We revealed. Ask the People of the Reminder if you do not know. We did not make them bodies that did not eat food, nor were they immortal. (21:7-8)

God's Help to the Prophets

One of the divine precedents in history is that God helps His prophets and comes to their aid with unforeseen relief. According to this divine tradition, the ultimate victory is that of the prophets. Of course, prophets and the faithful may face hardship at some point and suffer, but they will eventually achieve the ultimate victory and truth will overcome falsehood. These verses clearly emphasize this fact.

☐ Apostles were certainly denied before you, yet they patiently bore being denied and tormented until Our help came to them. Nothing can change the words of God, and there have certainly come to you some of the accounts of the apostles. (6:34)

☐ Do you suppose that you will enter paradise though there has not yet come to you the like of what befell those who went before you? Stress and distress befell them and they were convulsed until the apostle and the faithful who were with him said, 'When will God's help come?' Behold! God's help is indeed near! (2:214)

☐ Certainly Our decree has gone beforehand in favour of Our servants, the apostles, that they will indeed receive God's help, and indeed Our hosts will be the victors. (37:171-173)

☐ We shall indeed help Our apostles and those who have faith in the life of the world and on the day when the witnesses rise up, (40:51)

☐ We shall cast terror into the hearts of the faithless because of their ascribing partners to God, for which He has not sent down any authority, and their refuge shall be the Fire, and evil is the final abode of the wrongdoers.' (3:151)

The Prophet's Proofs and Arguments

The divine prophets had miracles and proofs to prove their truthfulness. Sometimes they engaged in argument with the deniers and disbelievers, giving clear reasons, which sometimes convinced the other side and sometimes it remained in denial.

The prophets used reason and logic in their arguments and sometimes appealed to the human conscience and rational sentiments.

The prophets, as stated in the selected verses, used different methods of persuasion, depending on which method was most effective in each case.

☐ Their apostles said, 'Is there any doubt about God, the originator of the heavens and the earth?! He calls you to forgive you a part of your sins, and grants you respite until a specified time.'

They said, 'You are nothing but humans like us who desire to bar us from what our fathers used to worship. So bring us a clear authority.' (14:10)

☐ But the elite of the faithless from among his people said, 'We do not see you to be anything but a human being like ourselves, and we do not see anyone following you except the simple-minded riff raff from our midst. Nor do we see that you have any merit over us. Indeed, we consider you to be liars.'

He said, 'O my people! Tell me, should I stand on a clear proof from my Lord, and He has granted me His own mercy—though it should be lost on you—shall we force it upon you while you are averse to it? (11:27-28)

☐ They said, 'We worship idols, and we keep on attending to them.'

He said, 'Do they hear you when you call them? Or do they bring you any benefit, or cause you any harm?'

They said, 'Indeed, we found our fathers doing likewise.'

He said, 'Have you regarded what you have been worshipping, you and your ancestors? They are indeed enemies to me, but the Lord of all the nations, (26:71-77)

☐ Have you not regarded him who argued with Abraham about his Lord, only because God had given him kingdom? When Abraham said, 'My Lord is He who gives life and brings death,' he replied, 'I too give life and bring death.' Abraham said, 'God indeed brings the sun from the east; now you bring it from the west.' Thereat the faithless one was dumbfounded. And God does not guide the wrongdoing lot. (2:258)

☐ His people argued with him. He said, 'Do you argue with me concerning God, while He has guided me for certain? I do not fear what you ascribe to Him as His partners, excepting anything that my Lord may wish. My Lord embraces all things in His knowledge. Will you not then take admonition?'

'How could I fear what you ascribe to Him as partners, when you do not fear ascribing partners to God for which He has not sent down any authority to you? So tell me, which of the two sides has a greater right to safety, if you know? (6:80-81)

⮞ Certainly We gave Abraham his rectitude aforetime, and We knew him when he said to his father and his people, 'What are these images to which you keep on attending?'

They said, 'We found our fathers worshipping them.'

He said, 'Certainly you and your fathers have been in plain error.'

They said, 'Are you telling the truth,b or are you just kidding?'

He said, 'Your Lord is indeed the Lord of the heavens and the earth, who originated them, and I bear witness to this. By God, I will devise a stratagem against your idols after you have gone away.'

So he broke them into pieces, all except the biggest of them, so that they might come back to it.

They said, 'Whoever has done this to Our gods?! He is indeed a wrongdoer!'

They said, 'We heard a young man speaking ill of them. He is called "Abraham." '

They said, 'Bring him before the people's eyes so that they may bear witness against him.'

They said, 'Was it you who did this to our gods, O Abraham?'

He said, 'No, it was this biggest one of them who did it! Ask them, if they can speak.'

Thereat they came to themselves and said to one another, 'It is you indeed who are the wrongdoers!' Then they hung their heads. However, they said, 'You certainly know that they cannot speak.'

He said, 'Then, do you worship besides God that which cannot cause you any benefit or harm? Fie on you and what you worship besides God! Do you not exercise your reason?' (21:51-67)

⮞ Invite to the way of your Lord with wisdom and good

advice and dispute with them in a manner that is best. Indeed, your Lord knows best those who stray from His way, and He knows best those who are guided. (16:125)

Mockery and Persecution of the Prophets

The opposition had nothing to say in response to the clear evidence and solid arguments of the prophets. But as a result of antagonism and obstinacy, they continued to insist on their denial and to take resort to inhuman methods to pursue their ends. One was to ridicule the prophets with the aim of bringing down their personality in the eyes of the people. Another was to torture and persecute them and the believers, so that others would not turn to the prophets for fear of torture.

☐ Apostles were certainly denied before you, yet they patiently bore being denied and tormented until Our help came to them.
Nothing can change the words of God, and there have certainly come to you some of the accounts of the apostles. (6:34)

☐ When Moses said to his people, 'O my people! Why do you torment me, when you certainly know that I am God's apostle to you?' So when they swerved from the right path, God made their hearts swerve, and God does not guide the transgressing lot. (61:5)

☐ Indeed, those who offend God and His Apostle are cursed by God in the world and the Hereafter, and He has prepared a humiliating punishment for them. (33:57)

☐ Apostles were certainly derided before you; but those who ridiculed them were besieged by what they had been deriding. (21:41)

☐ How regrettable of the servants! There did not come to

them any apostle but that they used to deride him. (36:30)

▢ That is how We let it pass through the hearts of the guilty: (15:12-12)

The Prophetic Mission

The most important mission of the prophets was to propagate the religion and spread God's message among the people. In this path they spared no effort and worked tirelessly with all their being, fearing no one. The duty assigned to them was to communicate their message, regardless of whether the people were influenced or not. The prophets always performed this duty in a variety of ways with compassion and benevolence, and sometimes faced strong opposition from the deniers, but their hostility and opposition did not affect their resolution to carry out their duty.

These facts are clearly reflected in the following verses.

▢ If you impugn the Apostle's teaching, then other nations have impugned likewise before you, and the Apostle's duty is only to communicate in clear terms. (29:18)

▢ —Such as deliver the messages of God and fear Him and fear no one except God, and God suffices as reckoner. (33:39)

▢ Obey God and obey the Apostle, and beware; but if you turn your backs, then know that Our Apostle's duty is only to communicate in clear terms. (5:92)

▢ He said, 'O my people, I am not in error. Rather, I am an apostle from the Lord of all the nations. (7:61)

▢ This is a Book that has been sent down to you and as admonition for the faithful; so let there be no disquiet in your heart on its account that you may warn thereby. (7:2)

☐ And mention Hūd, the brother of ʿĀd, when he warned his people at Ahqāf—and warners have passed away before and after him—saying, 'Do not worship anyone but God. I indeed fear for you the punishment of a tremendous day.'

They said, 'Have you come to turn us away from our gods? Then bring us what you threaten us with, if you are truthful.

He said, 'Its knowledge is with God alone, and I communicate to you what I have been sent with. But I see that you are an ignorant lot.' (46:21-23)

☐ But if they disregard your warnings, remember that We have not sent you as their keeper. Your duty is only to communicate.

Indeed, when We let man taste Our mercy, he boasts about it; but should an ill visit them because of what their hands have sent ahead, then man is very ungrateful. (42:48)

The Teachings of the Prophets

In their preaching, the prophets communicated to the people the sublime knowledge and ordinances, and in general the law that they had received through divine revelation, without adding anything from themselves. They propagated monotheism and worship of God, social unity, self-cultivation of and contemplation in divine works, justice, charity and values of this kind. Here are some examples of their teachings in these verses:

☐ Certainly We raised an apostle in every nation to preach: 'Worship God and shun satanic entities.' Among them were some whom God guided, and among them were some who deserved to be in error. So travel through the land and observe how was the fate of the deniers. (16:36)

☐ Their apostles said to them, 'We are indeed just human

beings like yourselves; but God favours whomever of His servants that He wishes. We may not bring you an authority except by God's leave, and in God alone let all the faithful put their trust. (14:11)

☐ Certainly We sent Our apostles with clear proofs, and We sent down with them the Book and the Balance, so that mankind may maintain justice; and We sent down iron, in which there is great might and uses for mankind, and so that God may know those who help Him and His apostles with faith in the Unseen. God is indeed all-strong, all-mighty. (57:25)

☐ They did not divide into sects except after the knowledge had come to them, out of envy among themselves; and were it not for a prior decree of your Lord granting them reprieve until a specified time, decision would have been made between them. Indeed, those who were made heirs to the Book after them are in grave doubt concerning it. (42:14)

☐ It does not behoove any human that God should give him the Book, judgement and prophethood, and then he should say to the people, 'Be my servants instead of God.' Rather he would say, 'Be a godly people, because of your teaching the Book and because of your studying it.' (3:79)

☐ To the people of Midian We sent Shu'ayb, their townsman. He said, 'O my people, worship God! You have no other god besides Him. There has come to you a clear proof from your Lord. Observe fully the measure and the balance, do not cheat the people of their goods,c and do not cause corruption in the land after its restoration. That is better for you, if you are faithful. And do not lie in wait on every road to threaten and bar those who have faith in Him from the way of God, seeking to make it crooked. Remember when you were few and He multiplied you, and observe how was the fate of the agents of corruption. (7:85-86)

☐ Even as We sent to you an Apostle from among yourselves, who recites to you Our signs and purifies you, and teaches you the Book and wisdom, and teaches you what you did not know. (2:151)

☐ We did not send down the Book to you except for the purpose that you may clarify for them what they differ about, and as guidance and mercy for people who have faith. (16:64)

☐ We did not send any apostles before you except as men to whom We revealed. Ask the People of the Reminder if you do not know. We sent them with clear proofs and scriptures. We have sent down the Reminder to you so that you may clarify for these people that which has been sent down to them, so that they may reflect. (16:43-44)

Enemies of the Prophets and Gainsayers

Because the teachings of the prophets were incompatible with the interests of some individuals in the community, they stood up and opposed the prophets. Other people opposed them, not for the sake of material gain, but because of ignorance and imitation of their ancestors. In any case, there were groups who opposed them and prevented them from spreading their teachings and did not hesitate to suppress them. Their opposition was sometimes through denial, sometimes ridicule, sometimes intimidation, sometimes through scepticism and sometimes through war. This conflict between the prophets and the disbelievers was in fact a continuing conflict between right and wrong. Some features of this constant confrontation are reflected In these verses:

☐ That is how for every prophet We have assigned the devils from among humans and jinn as enemies, who inspire each other with seductive statements to deceive the people. Had your Lord wished, they would not have done it. So leave them with what they fabricate, (6:112)

☐ We did not send any warner to a town without its affluent ones saying, 'We indeed disbelieve in what you have been sent with.' (34:34)

☐ Then We sent Our apostles successively. Whenever there came to a nation its apostle, they impugned him, so We made them follow one another to extinction and We turned them into folk-tales. So away with the faithless lot! (23:44)

☐ If they impugn you, those before them have impugned likewise: their apostles brought them manifest proofs, holy writs, and illuminating scriptures. (35:25)

☐ Certainly We gave Moses the Book and followed him with the apostles, and We gave Jesus, the son of Mary, clear proofs and confirmed him with the Holy Spirit.
Is it not that whenever an apostle brought you that which was not to your liking, you would act arrogantly; so you would impugn a group of them, and slay another group? (2:87)

☐ But the faithless said to their apostles, 'Surely we will expel you from our land, or you shall revert to our creed.'
Thereat their Lord revealed to them: 'We will surely destroy the wrongdoers, (14:13)

☐ They are the ones who deny the signs of their Lord and encounter with Him. So their works have failed. On the Day of Resurrection We will not give them any weight. That is their requital—hell—because of their unfaith and their deriding My signs and My apostles. (18:105-106)

Miracles of the Prophets

The divine prophets presented clear proofs, one of the

most important of which were miracles, to prove their truthfulness and that they were inspired by God. A miracle is a wonderful work that others are not capable of carrying out, even if they were to assist each other. The miracles of the prophets were varied and usually based on the requirements of the time. For example, Moses, who lived in an age of sorcery and great magicians, offered miracles that appeared to be like magic, and magicians confessed to their incapacity against him. Or Jesus, who was lived during an age of progress in medicine in Greece, performed miracles of healing, resurrecting the dead and healed the born blind—things that medicine is incapable of doing. Similarly, the miracle of the Prophet of Islam, was of literary kind. The Qur'an was revealed in an age of flourishing eloquence and great poets, who confessed to the miraculous eloquence and rhetoric of the Qur'an. They were powerless to produce its like.

The verses selected describe some miracles of the various prophets.

☐ He said, 'If you have brought a sign, produce it, if you are truthful.'
Thereat he threw down his staff, and behold, it became a manifest python. Then he drew out his hand, and behold, it was bright and white to the onlookers. (7:106-108)

☐ They said, 'Burn him and help your gods, if you are to do anything!'
We said, 'O fire! Be cool and safe for Abraham!' They plotted to harm him, but We made them the biggest losers. (21:68-70)

☐ When God will say, O Jesus son of Mary, remember My blessing upon you and upon your mother, when I strengthened you with the Holy Spirit, so you would speak to the people in the cradle and in adulthood, and when I taught you the Book and wisdom, the Torah and the Gospel, and when you would create from clay the form of a bird with My leave, and you would breathe into it and it would become a bird with My leave; and you would heal the blind and the leper with My leave, and you would raise the dead with My leave; and when I held off the evil of the Children of Israel from you when you brought them clear proofs, whereat the faithless among them said, 'This is nothing but plain magic.' (5:110)

☐ So We revealed to him: 'Build the ark before Our eyes and by Our revelation. When Our edict comes and the oven gushes a stream of water, bring into it a pair of every kind of animal, and your family, except those of them against whom the decree has gone beforehand, and do not plead with Me for those who are wrongdoers: they shall indeed be drowned.' 'When you, and those who are with you, are settled in the ark, say, "All praise belongs to God, who has delivered us from the wrongdoing lot." And say, "My Lord! Land me with a blessed landing, for You are the best of those who bring ashore." '
There are indeed signs in this; and indeed We have been testing. (23:27-30)

☐ And when Moses prayed for water for his people, We said, 'Strike the rock with your staff.' Thereat twelve fountains gushed forth from it; every tribe came to know its drinking-place. 'Eat and drink of God's provision, and do not act wickedly on the earth, causing corruption.' (2:60)

☐ And when We parted the sea with you,a and We delivered you and drowned Pharaoh's clan as you looked on. (2:50)

☐ And if you are in doubt concerning what We have sent down to Our servant, then bring a sūrah like it, and invoke your helpers besides God, if you are truthful. But if you do not—and you will not—then beware the Fire whose fuel will be humans and stones, prepared for the faithless. (2:23-24)

Chapter 5

Prophet Muhammad

The Qur'an on the Prophecies in Torah & the Gospel

No informed student of world history can deny that in its entire recorded course no religious-cultural movement has had such a spectacular appearance and forceful impact on human civilization and was followed by such sustained, pervasive and progressive world-wide influence, as Islam at its advent in seventh century Arabia, one of the most unlikeliest of places. Never before the Prophet Muhammad, nor since, has the phenomenon of prophecy ever been staged with such grandeur and on such a grand scale and with such far-reaching consequences for human civilization. Never before had a prophet written letters to emperors and rulers informing them of his prophethood and inviting them to his creed as the Prophet did to Heraclius the Byzantine Emperor, Khusroes the Persian monarch and Muqawqis, the ruler of Idolatry and worship of pagan gods, an ever-present feature of the Middle-Eastern civilizations of antiquity disappeared for ever under the impact of his teaching and efforts, not only from Arabia but also the entire Middle East and many other parts of the world.

For those who believe in the prophecies of the past sages, his appearance had been foretold repeatedly in the former scriptures, especially those related to the Abrahamic tradition.

The Qur'an itself asserts that the mission of the Prophet as a great turning point in the destiny of mankind had been anticipated by the prophets of old since the era of the Patriarchs. It portrays Abraham and Ishmael as praying for his appearance as they raised the foundations of the Ka'bah:

> As Abraham raised the foundations of the House with Ishmael, they prayed: 'Our Lord, accept it from us! Indeed, You are the All-hearing, the All-knowing … Our Lord, raise amongst them (that is, in their progeny) an apostle from among them, who will recite to them Your signs and teach them the Book and wisdom and purify them. Indeed, You are the All-mighty, the All-wise.' (2:127, 129)

Elsewhere, Moses is portrayed as receiving from God the good news of the advent of the greatest Apostle, whose mention the future followers of Moses will find written with them in the Torah and the Gospel:

> 'I visit My punishment on whomever I wish, but My mercy embraces all things. Soon I shall appoint it for those who are Godwary and give the *zakāt* and those who believe in Our signs —those who follow the Apostle, the untaught prophet, whose mention they find written with them in the Torah and the Gospel, who bids them to do what is right and forbids them from what is wrong, makes lawful to them all the good things and forbids them from all vicious things, and relieves them of their burdens and the shackles that were upon them—those who believe in him, honour him, and help him and follow the

light that has been sent down with him, they are the felicitous.' (7:156-157)

☐ Muhammad, the Apostle of God, and those who are with him are hard against the faithless and merciful amongst themselves. You see them bowing and prostrating in worship, seeking God's grace and His pleasure. Their mark is visible on their faces, from the effect of prostration. Such is their description in the Torah and their description in the Gospel: like a tillage that sends out its shoots and builds them up, and they grow stout and settle on their stalks, impressing the sowers, so that He may enrage the faithless by them. (48:29)

The Qur'an also cites Jesus Christ, who, while he confirmed the extant Torah, gave the good news of a future messenger:

☐ And when Jesus son of Mary said, 'O Children of Israel! I am indeed the apostle of God to you, to confirm what is before me of the Torah and to give good news of an apostle who will come after me, whose name is Ahmad.' (61:6)

Prophet Muhammad in the Hebrew Bible

We did not send you but as mercy to all the nations. (21:107)

Islamic sources and Muslim scholars have identified passages in the Hebrew Bible which appear to anticipate the appearance of a great leader-prophet who will play an unprecedented role in the religious and political destiny of mankind. In the Judaic tradition, since pre-Christian times, that future prophet-ruler came to be identified in the popular imagination as 'the Messiah,' who, the Israelites believed, will be born in the descent of David. The same title was applied to Jesus by his Jewish followers in anticipation of a time when he would return to rule the world.

But first let's deal with these prophecies in a chronological order. The Divine promise given to Abraham for his faith and obedience plays a singular role in the history of the Abrahamic traditions. When Abraham had gone through the ordeal of sacrificing his 'only son' for the love of God, he was given the promise that through his 'offspring all nations on earth would be blessed.' Muslim scholars argue that the words 'only son' can only be true of Ishmael, who was Abraham's first-born. Moreover, the prophets of the progeny of Isaac and Jacob—including Jesus[1]—preached to the Israelites. Other nations were never part of their prophetic agenda.

> The angel of the Lord called to Abraham from heaven a second time and said, "I swear by myself, declares the Lord, that because you have done this and have not withheld your son, your only son, I will surely bless you and make your descendants as numerous as the stars in the sky and as the sand on the seashore. Your descendants will take possession of the cities of their enemies, and *through your offspring all nations on earth will be blessed,* because you have obeyed me." (Genesis 22:15-18)

It is well known that kingly power and authority with religious sanction among the Israelites did reside for a few generations in the house of David, who belonged to the tribe of Judah. At the end of the Book of Genesis, Jacob is reported as addressing and blessing his sons. Jacob blesses Judah with the following words, which indicate

---

[1] "I was sent only to the lost sheep of Israel …" "It is not right to take the children's bread and toss it to their dogs." (Math. 15:24, 26; see also Mark 7:27)

that he foresaw a time when self-rule under a divinely sanctioned ruler will depart from the Israelites and pass into the hands of 'him to whom it belongs and who enjoys the obedience of nations.'

> "Judah, your brothers will praise you; your hand will be on the neck of your enemies; your father's sons will bow down to you … The sceptre will not depart from Judah, nor the ruler's staff from between his feet, until he comes to whom it belongs and the obedience of the nations is his." (Genesis 49:8-10)

History knows of no greater prophet-ruler -lawgiver than the Apostle of God, obedience to whom cane to be considered obligatory by all the nations known to the Israelites and inhabiting Palestine and the surrounding regions and, in the course of time, many communities inhabiting the five continents.

A key expression in this passage is 'the obedience of nations.' As mentioned above, the mission of the Israelite prophets from Moses to Jesus was directed towards the Israelites. All the books of the Hebrew Bible testify to this fact. An apparent exception is Jonah, who was sent solely to the people of Nineveh, in Mesopotamia, and he can hardly be said to have held the sceptre or enjoy 'the obedience of nations.'

More significant and focussed is the following passage from Deuteronomy, where God is described as telling Moses that he "will raise a prophet like you" from among the *brothers* of the Israelites. There has been no other prophet like the Apostle of God, who resembled Moses in several ways. Both of them were lawgivers, leaders and rulers of their people and brought scriptures for which there is no other counterpart in world history. Evidently,

Jesus was not that prophet, as he was neither a ruler nor leader of his people and he followed the Mosaic Law. He never claimed to be that prophet, and his disciples looked to his second coming for the fulfilment of the above-mentioned prophecy. His preaching was limited to the Jews and he declared that he was sent only to the 'lost sheep of Israel,' as is clear from his response to the request of the Canaanite woman.

The following prophecy is from Moses:

> The Lord your God will raise up *for you* a prophet like me *from among your own brothers*. You must listen to him … The Lord said to me: "… I will raise up *for them* (i.e. the Israelites) a prophet like you *from among their brothers*;[1] I will put my words in his mouth, and he will tell them everything I command him. If anyone does not listen to my words that the prophet speaks in my name, I myself will call him to account. (Deuteronomy 18:15, 17-19)

The words 'for you; and 'for them' obviously refer to the Israelites, and the expressions 'from your own brothers' and ' from their brothers' obviously indicate that the promised prophet would not be an Israelite.

There is another statement said to be made by Moses

---

[1] The Hebrew wording in verses 15 and 18 is *'from among your own brothers'* (מִקִּרְבְּךָ מֵאַחֶיךָ) and *from among their brothers'* (מִקֶּרֶב אֲחֵיהֶם), respectively, as given above from the New International Version. However, NRSV alters the translation as follows: '[a prophet like me] from among your own people,' and '[a prophet like you] from among their own people.' The JPS translation of the Hebrew Bible translates the wording in vv 15 and 18 as follows: '[a prophet] from among your own people, [like myself],' and '[a prophet for them] from among their own people, [like yourself].' The King James Bible has these respective renderings for the verses: 'a Prophet from the midst of thee, of thy brethren, like unto me,' and 'a Prophet from among their brethren, like unto thee.'

himself before his death. In a short sentence, he summarily refers to three great prophetic missions, his own and those of Jesus and the Prophet Muhammad, the last of which is described as 'the shining forth of the Lord from Mount Paran' ('Paran' is a biblical term used in its oldest usage for Mecca, the place where Ishmael, the Prophet's ancestor, lived and which is referred to in Gen. 21:21: 'He lived in the desert and became an archer. While he was living in the Desert of Paran, his mother got a wife for him from Egypt.)

> This is the blessing that Moses the man of God pronounced on the Israelites before his death. He said: "The Lord came from Sinai and dawned over them from Seir; he shone forth from Mount Paran. He came with myriads of holy ones from the south, from his mountain slopes. (Deuteronomy 33:1-2)

Then there is the long prophesy in Isaiah about the 'chosen servant' of God, who will 'bring justice to nations'—not merely to the Israelites—'in whose law the islands will put their hope,' who will be 'a covenant for the people and a light to the Gentiles'—not merely to the Hebrews—who will 'open eyes that are blind,' 'free captives from prison' and 'release from the dungeons those who sit in darkness,' at whose appearance the settlements of Kedar (that is, those of the Ishmaelites) will rejoice, who 'will march out like a mighty man' and 'triumph over his enemies.' Those who are familiar with the accounts of the Hebrew prophets along with the early history of Islam will confirm that this description fits only the unique figure of the Apostle of God, who was a paragon of gentleness and forgiveness while being the prophet-warrior:

> "Here is my servant, whom I uphold, my chosen one

in whom delight; I will put my Spirit on him and he will bring justice to the nations. He will not shout or cry out, or raise his voice in the streets.

A bruised reed he will not break, and a smouldering wick he will not snuff out. In faithfulness he will bring forth justice; he will not falter or be discouraged till he establishes justice on earth. In his law the islands will put their hope."

This is what God the Lord says—he who created the heavens and stretched them out, who spread out the earth and all that comes out of it, who gives breath to its people, and life to those who walk on it:

"I, the Lord , have called you in righteousness; I will take hold of your hand. I will keep you and will make you to be a covenant for the people and a light for the Gentiles, to open eyes that are blind, to free captives from prison and to release from the dungeon those who sit in darkness.

"I am the Lord; that is my name! I will not give my glory to another or my praise to idols. See, the former things have taken place, and new things I declare; before they spring into being I announce them to you." Sing to the Lord a new song, his praise from the ends of the earth, you who go down to the sea, and all that is in it, you islands, and all who live in them.

Let the desert and its towns raise their voices; let the settlements where Kedar lives rejoice. Let the people of Sela sing for joy; let them shout from the mountaintops. Let them give glory to the Lord and proclaim his praise in the islands.

The Lord will march out like a mighty man, like a warrior he will stir up his zeal; with a shout he will raise the battle cry and will triumph over his enemies… " I will lead the blind by ways they have not known, along unfamiliar paths I will guide them; I will turn the darkness into light before them and make the rough places smooth. These are the things I will do; I will not forsake them. But those who trust in idols, who say to images, 'You are our gods,' will be turned back in utter shame. Israel Blind and Deaf "Hear, you deaf; look, you blind, and see! (Isaiah 42:1-17)

> Then there is the prophecy of Habakkuk. Like the aforementioned vision of Moses about the Lord shining forth from Mount Paran, the vision of Habakkuk also presages the advent of a mighty prophetic figure before whom the ancient pagan traditions would crumble and who will fill the earth with the Lord's praise through the prayer he will teach and institute:

☐ God came from Teman, the Holy One from Mount Paran. Selah His glory covered the heavens and his praise filled the earth. His splendour was like the sunrise; rays flashed from his hand, where his power was hidden … He stood, and shook the earth; he looked, and made the nations tremble. The ancient mountains crumbled and the age-old hills collapsed. His ways are eternal. (Habakkuk 3:3-6)

> Haggai in his prophecy holds out the promise of the Prophet of Peace, 'the desired of all nations,' who will come to God's house—meaning either the Ka'bah, whose glory exceeds that of any house ever built for God's worship, or the al-Aqsa Mosque in Jerusalem, which was visited by the Holy Prophet during his nocturnal celestial journey:

☐ "This is what the Lord Almighty says: 'In a little while[1] I will once more shake the heavens and the earth, the sea and the

---

[1] "In a little while" is to be understood in the light of the reminder in 2 Peter 3:8-9: "But do not forget this one thing, dear friends: With the Lord a day is like a thousand years, and a thousand years are like a day. The Lord is not slow in keeping his promise, as some understand slowness. He is patient with you, not wanting anyone to perish, but everyone to come to repentance."

dry land. I will shake all nations, and the desired of all nations will come, and I will fill this house with glory,' says the Lord Almighty.

'The silver is mine and the gold is mine,' declares the Lord Almighty. 'The glory of this present house will be greater than the glory of the former house,' says the Lord Almighty. 'And in this place I will grant peace,' declares the Lord Almighty." (Haggai 2:6-9)

Malachi also prophecies the advent of "the messenger of the covenant" who "will be like a refiner's fire", and who will come suddenly to the Temple and whose followers shall bring offerings in righteousness:

> "See, I will send my messenger, who will prepare the way before me. *Then suddenly the lord you are seeking will come to his temple; the messenger of the covenant, whom you desire, will come,*" says the Lord Almighty. But who can endure the day of his coming? Who can stand when he appears? *For he will be like a refiner's fire or a launderer's soap. He will sit as a refiner and purifier of silver;* he will purify the Levites and refine them like gold and silver. Then the Lord will have men who will bring offerings in righteousness, (Malachi 3:1-3)

Daniel in his vision beholds an exalted human being who is presented to the Almighty and who is given an everlasting sovereignty and whose people, the holy ones of the Most High, shall be served and obeyed by all dominions on earth:

> As I looked on, in the night vision, one like a human being came with the clouds of heaven. He reached the Ancient of Days and was presented to Him. Dominion, glory, and kingship were given to him. His dominion is an everlasting dominion that shall not pass away, and his kingship, one that shall not

be destroyed ... The kingship and dominion and grandeur belonging to all the kingdoms under Heaven will be given to the people of the holy ones of the Most High. Their kingdom shall be an everlasting kingdom and all dominions shall serve and obey them. (Daniel 7:13-14, 27, Tanakh, JPS, 1985)

> These passages are reminiscent of the Qur'anic verse: Certainly We wrote in the Psalms, after the Torah: 'My righteous servants shall indeed inherit the earth.' There is indeed in this a proclamation for a devout people. (21:105)

Prophet Muhammad in the New Testament

Zechariah, the father of John the Baptist and, according to the Qur'an, a mentor and guardian to Mary, the mother of Jesus, is referred to as a mere ' priest' in the Christian scripture.[1] He is, however, considered a prophetic figure in the Qur'an, who sees his son's future mission as preparing the way for the "rising sun ... to guide our feet into the path of peace:"

> His (i.e., John's) father Zechariah was filled with the Holy Spirit and prophesied: "Praise be to the Lord, the God of Israel, because he has come and has redeemed his people. He has raised up a horn of salvation for us in the house of his servant David ...
> And you, my child, will be called a prophet of the Most High; *for you will go on before the Lord to prepare the way for him, to give his people the knowledge of salvation through the forgiveness of their sins, because of the tender mercy of our God, by which the rising sun will come to us from heaven to shine on those living in darkness and in the shadow of death, to guide our feet into the path of peace.*" (Luke 1:67-69; 76-79)

[1] Luke 1:5.

Later, John himself is reported as referring to the future messenger in terms reminiscent of the words of Malachi ('he will be like a refiner's fire'):

> "I baptise you with water for repentance. But after me will come one who is more powerful than I, whose sandals I am not fit to carry. He will baptise you with the Holy Spirit and with fire. *His winnowing fork is in his hand, and he will clear his threshing floor, gathering his wheat into the barn and burning up the chaff with unquenchable fire.*" (Matthew 3:11-12; cf. Luke 3:16)

"After me" cannot possibly refer to Jesus, who was John's cousin and only six months his junior. Moreover, Jesus himself had been baptised by John, and as one writer has pointed out, "If Jesus were in reality the person whom the Baptist foretold as 'more powerful' than himself, so much so that he was 'not worthy to kneel and unloose his shoes,' and that 'he would baptise with the Spirit and fire,' there would be no necessity nor any sense in his being baptised by his inferior in the river like an ordinary penitent Jew.[1]

Moreover, Jesus himself is depicted as making a similar statement in the Gospel of Barnabas concerning the greatness of the future messenger:

> "I am a voice that cries through all Judea, and cries: 'Prepare ye the way for the messenger of the Lord,' even as it is written in Esaias… The miracles which God worketh by my hands show that I speak that which God wills; nor indeed do I make myself to be accounted as him of whom you speak. For I am not worthy to unloose the ties of the hosen or the ratchets of the shoes of the Messenger of God whom you call "Messiah," who was made before me, and shall come after me, and shall

---

[1] Abdul Ahad Dawud (AKA David Benjamin Keldani), *Muhammad in the Bible* (Penerbitan Pustaka Antara, 1987), p. 160.

bring the words of truth, so that his faith shall have no end." (Gospel of Barnabas, pp. 97-99)

☐ "As for me, I am now come to the world to prepare the way for the messenger of God, who shall bring salvation to the world. But beware that ye be not deceived, for many false prophets shall come, who shall take my words and contaminate my gospel." (Gospel of Barnabas, p. 167)

> The Gospel of Barnabas is dismissed as a Muslim forgery by Christian scholars, but the prophecies of Jesus about the future 'Comforter' or 'Counselor' (Greek: parákletos) as reported in the following passages from John, the latest and most theologically wrought of the four Gospels that incorporates the incipient theology of the Logos and the Holy Spirit, clearly echo his statements about the Prophet Muhammad as they appear in the Qur'an (61:6):

☐ And I will ask the Father, and he will give you another Counsellor to be with you forever—the Spirit of truth. (John 14:16-17)

☐ But the Counsellor, the Holy Spirit, whom the Father will send in my name, will teach you all things and will remind you of everything I have said to you ... (John 14:26)

☐ When the Counsellor comes, whom I will send to you from the Father, the Spirit of truth who goes out from the Father, he will testify about me ... (John 15:26)

☐ But I tell you the truth: It is for your good that I am going away. Unless I go away, the Counsellor will not come to you; but if I go, I will send him to you. When he comes, he will convict the world of guilt in regard to sin and righteousness and judgment: in regard to sin, because men do not believe in me; in regard to righteousness, because I am going to the Father, where you can see me no longer; and in regard to judgment, because the prince of this world now stands condemned. I have much more to say to you, more than you can now bear. But when he, the Spirit of truth, comes, he will guide you into all truth. He will not speak on his own; he will speak only what he hears,[1] and he will tell you what is yet to come. (John 16:7-13)

Prophet Muhammad in the Qur'an

☐ Say, 'I am not a novelty among the apostles, nor do I know what will be done with me or with you. I just follow whatever is revealed to me, and I am just a manifest warner.' (46:9)

☐ Say, 'If you love God, then follow me; God will love you and forgive you your sins, and God is all-forgiving, all-merciful.' Say, 'Obey God and the Apostle.' But if they turn away, indeed God does not like the faithless. (3:31-32)

☐ Never will the Jews be pleased with you, nor the Christians, unless you followed their creed. Say, 'Indeed, it is the guidance of God which is the true guidance.' And should you follow their base desires after the knowledge that has come to you, you will not have against God any friend or helper. (2:120)

☐ Say, 'We have faith in God and in what has been sent down to us, and what was sent down to Abraham, Ishmael, Isaac, Jacob and the Tribes, and what Moses, Jesus and the prophets were given by their Lord. We make no distinction between any

---

[1] 'He will not speak on his own; he will speak only what he hears,' these words do not sound as possibly applying to the Holy Spirit, conceived by Christian theology as God and one of the persons of the Trinity. They remind one, in fact, of the description Moses is reported to have given in his prophecy of the future prophet, 'I will put my words in his mouth, and he will tell them everything I command him.' A similar statement is made in the Qur'an about Prophet Muhammad. 'He does not speak out of [his own] desire: it is just a revelation that is revealed [to him]' (53:3-4)

of them, and to Him do we submit.'

Should anyone follow a religion other than Islam, it shall never be accepted from him, and he will be among the losers in the Hereafter. (3:84-85)

☐ They say, 'Be either Jews or Christians so that you may be rightly guided.' Say, 'No, rather we will follow the creed of Abraham, a *hanīf*, and he was not one of the polytheists.'

Say, 'We have faith in God and that which has been sent down to us, and that which was sent down to Abraham, Ishmael, Isaac, Jacob and the Tribes, then know that they are only steeped in defiance. God shall suffice you against them, and He is the All-hearing, the All-knowing.

'The baptism of God, and who baptises better than God? And Him do we worship.'

Say, 'Will you argue with us concerning God, while He is our Lord and your Lord, and to us our deeds belong, and to you your deeds belong, and we worship Him dedicatedly?'

Ask them, 'Do you say that Abraham, Ishmael, Isaac, Jacob, and the Tribes were Jews or Christians?' Say, 'Is it you who know better, or God?' And who is a greater wrongdoer than someone who conceals a testimony that is with him from God? And God is not oblivious of what you do. (2:135-140)

The Principles of His Invitation

The Prophet of Islam, as the last and greatest of divine envoys, brought the most complete religion to humankind. The content of his message for human guidance and prosperity was sufficient to the end of the world. He invited people to the knowledge of God, to light, wisdom and ethical values, and called them to avoid evil and indecent acts, cruelty and corruption. He taught all that was necessary for mankind's felicity in the world and the Hereafter, and his teaching was founded on insight, reasoning and wisdom.

He declared all good and healthy things lawful and forbade bad and harmful things, and liberated humankind from the chains of ignorance, superstition and error, and fought deviant traditions and ugly and irrational practices.

These verses are only examples of the vital teachings of Islam, and one must carefully study the entire Qur'an for further awareness in this regard.

> Say, 'O People of the Book! Come to a common word between us and you: that we will worship no one but God, that we will not ascribe any partner to Him, and that some of us will not take some others as lords besides God.' But if they turn away, say, 'Be witnesses that we have submitted to God.' (3:64)

> [T]hose who follow the Apostle, the untaught prophet, whose mention they find written with them in the Torah and the Gospel, who bids them to do what is right and forbids them from what is wrong, makes lawful to them all the good things and forbids them from all vicious things, and relieves them of their burdens and the shackles that were upon them—those who believe in him, honour him, and help him and follow the light that has been sent down with him, they are the felicitous.' (7:157)

> Say, 'Come, I will recount what your Lord has forbidden you: That you shall not ascribe any partners to Him, and you shall be good to the parents, you shall not kill your children due to penury—We will provide for you and for them—you shall not approach indecencies, the outward among them and the inward ones, and you shall not kill a soul whose life God has made inviolable, except with due cause. This is what He has enjoined upon you so that you may exercise your reason. (6:151)

☐ Invite to the way of your Lord with wisdom and good advice and dispute with them in a manner that is best. Indeed, your Lord knows best those who stray from His way, and He knows best those who are guided. (16:125)

☐ There is no compulsion in religion: rectitude has become distinct from error. So one who disavows satanic entities and has faith in God has held fast to the firmest handle for which there is no breaking; and God is all-hearing, all-knowing. (2:256)

☐ O you who have faith! Answer God and the Apostle when he summons you to that which will give you life. Know that God intervenes between a man and his heart and that you will be mustered toward Him. (8:24)

☐ O you who have faith! Obey God and obey the Apostle and those vested with authority among you. And if you dispute concerning anything, refer it to God and the Apostle, if you have faith in God and the Last Day. That is better and more favourable in outcome. (4:59)

☐ Indeed, God enjoins justice and kindness, and generosity towards relatives, and He forbids indecency, wrongdoing, and aggression. He advises you so that you may take admonition.
Fulfil God's covenant when you pledge, and do not break your oaths after pledging them solemnly and having made God a witness over yourselves. God indeed knows what you do. (16:90-91)

☐ It is He who sent to the unlettered people an apostle from among themselves, to recite to them His signs, to purify them, and to teach them the Book and wisdom, and earlier they had indeed been in manifest error. (62:2)

☐ God invites to the abode of peace, and He guides whomever He wishes to a straight path.
Those who are virtuous shall receive the best reward and an enhancement. Neither dust nor abasement shall overcast their

faces. They shall be the inhabitants of paradise, and they shall remain in it forever.

⬜ For those who have committed misdeeds, the requital of a misdeed shall be its like, and they shall be overcast by abasement. They shall have no one to protect them from God. They will be as if their faces were covered with dark patches of the night. They shall be the inmates of the Fire, and they shall remain in it [forever]. (10:25-27)

The Prophet's Morals

The Prophet of Islam (peace be upon him) treated the people with kindness, compassion and good humour, so that one of the elements of his success in attracting people was his good morals. He was a mercy to the world and had a great character. He was commanded by God to be humble, pardoning and helping the people and calling them to virtue. The Prophet's compassion for the people and his concern for their proper guidance was so much that God warned him many times that he would perish out of his grief because of their lack of faith.

⬜ There has certainly come to you an apostle from among yourselves. Grievous to him is your distress; he has deep concern for you and is most kind and merciful to the faithful.
But if they turn their backs on you (O Prophet), say, 'God is sufficient for me. There is no god except Him. In Him alone I have put my trust and He is the Lord of the Great Throne.' (9:128-129)

⬜ It is by God's mercy that you (i.e., the Prophet) are gentle to them; had you been harsh and hard-hearted, they would have surely scattered from around you. So excuse them and plead for forgiveness for them, and consult them in the affairs, and once you are resolved, put your trust in God. Indeed, God loves those who trust in Him. (3:159)

☐ There is indeed in this (i.e., the Qur'an) a proclamation for a devout people. We did not send you (O Prophet) but as mercy to all the nations. (21:106-107)

☐ … Yours indeed will be an everlasting reward, and indeed you possess a great character. (68:3-4)

☐ Warn the nearest of your kinsfolk (O Prophet), and lower your wing to the faithful who follow you. (26:214-215)

☐ (O Prophet) adopt a policy of excusing the faults of people, bid what is right, and turn away from the ignorant.
Should a temptation from Satan disturb you, invoke the protection of God; indeed He is all-hearing, all-knowing. (7:199-200)

☐ Then We cursed them (i.e., the rebellious among the Israelites) because of their breaking their covenant and made their hearts hard: they pervert words from their meanings, and have forgotten a part of what they were reminded. You will not cease to learn of some of their treachery, excepting a few of them. Yet excuse them and forbear. Indeed, God loves the virtuous. (5:13)

☐ You are liable to imperil your life out of grief for their sake if they do not believe this discourse. (18:6)

Names and Titles of the Prophet in the Qur'an

The Holy Qur'an mentions the Prophet of Islam with specific names and titles. Among his names are 'Muhammad' and 'Ahmad,' and among his special titles and attributes, one finds the following: 'the Apostle,' 'the Prophet,' 'the Seal of the Prophets,' 'Ta Ha,' 'Ya Sin,' 'Mercy unto the nations,', 'the Trustworthy Counsellor,' 'the Herald of Good News,' 'the Warner,' 'the One Wrapped in His Mantle, 'the One covered in His Mantle,' etc., each of which has a specific meaning.

☐ Muhammad is not the father of any man among you, but he is the Apostle of God and the Seal of the Prophets, and God has knowledge of all things. (33:40)

☐ And when Jesus son of Mary said, 'O Children of Israel! I am indeed the apostle of God to you, to confirm what is before me of the Torah and to give good news of an apostle who will come after me, whose name is Ahmad.' But when he brought them clear proofs, they said, 'This is plain magic.' (61:6)

☐ We did not send you except as a bearer of good news and warner to all mankind, but most people do not know. (34:28)

☐ O Prophet! We have indeed sent you as a witness, as a bearer of good news and warner and as a summoner to God by His permission, and as a radiant lamp. (33:45-46)

☐ Whatever good befalls you is from God; and whatever ill befalls you is from yourself. We sent you as an apostle to mankind, and God suffices as witness. (4:79)

☐ Say, 'O mankind! I am the Apostle of God to you all, of Him to whom belongs the kingdom of the heavens and the earth. There is no god except Him. He gives life and brings death.' So have faith in God and His Apostle, the untaught prophet, who has faith in God and His words, and follow him so that you may be guided. (7:158)

☐ There is indeed in this a proclamation for a devout people. We did not send you but as mercy to all the nations. (21:106-107)

☐ Tā Hā! We did not send down the Qur'an to you that you should be miserable, but only as an admonition to him who fears his Lord. (20:1-3)

☐ Yā Sīn! By the Wise Qur'an, you are indeed one of the

apostles, on a straight path. (36:1-4)

☐ O you wrapped up in your mantle! Rise up and warn! Magnify your Lord, purify your clothes (74:1-4)

☐ O you wrapped up in your mantle! Stand vigil through the night, except for a little of it, a half, or reduce a little from that or add to it, and recite the Qur'an in a measured tone. (73:1-4)

Divine Help in the Prophet's life

The Prophet of Islam (Peace be upon him) enjoyed Divine support in his life from infancy to the end of his life, and God repeatedly assisted His Apostle in His wonderful ways, sometimes with direct help of the angels, sometimes with casting fear into the hearts of the enemies, sometimes with calm and composure in moments of crisis, and with other miraculous forms of help. He supported the Prophet and assured him so that he was always under God's protection and it is God who makes the guile of the enemies recoil upon themselves.

☐ If they incline toward peace, you too incline toward it and put your trust in God. Indeed, He is the All-hearing, the All-knowing. But if they desire to deceive you, God is indeed sufficient for you. It is He who strengthened you with His help and with the means of the faithful, and united their hearts. Had you spent all wealth that is on the earth, you could not have united their hearts, but God united them together. He is indeed all-mighty, all-wise.
O Prophet! Sufficient for you is God and those of the faithful who follow you. (8:61-64)

☐ If you (Muslims) do not help him, then God did certainly help him when the faithless expelled him as one of two refugees, when the two of them were in the cave, and he said to his companion, 'Do not grieve; God is indeed with us.' Then God sent down His composure upon him and strengthened him with hosts you did not see, and He made the word of the faithless the lowest, and the word of God is the highest, and God is all-mighty, all-wise. (9:40)

☐ So be patient (O Prophet)! God's promise is indeed true. And do not let yourself be upset by those who have no conviction. (30:60)

☐ So submit patiently to the judgement of your Lord, for indeed you (O Prophet) fare before Our eyes. And celebrate the praise of your Lord when you rise at dawn, and also glorify Him during the night and at the receding of the stars. (52:48-49)

☐ We shall cast terror into the hearts of the faithless because of their ascribing partners to God, for which He has not sent down any authority, and their refuge shall be the Fire, and evil is the final abode of the wrongdoers.' (3:151)

☐ God did not appoint it but as a good news for you and to reassure with it your hearts; and victory comes only from God, the All-mighty, the All-wise, that He may cut down a section of the faithless, or subdue them, so that they retreat disappointed. (3:126-127)

☐ —Those who set up another deity besides God. Soon they will know! (15:96)

The Obligation to Obey the Prophet

Obedience to the Prophet is obedience to God because everything he says in order to guide people and deliver God's commandments has been revealed to him by God. Since the Prophet of God is preserved from any error or slip, Muslims must submit to his commands and not dispute them, because everything he says is from God.

Anyone who loves God must obey His Prophet so that God may love him/her and place him/her in the ranks of His righteous and truthful servants for obeying the Prophet.

The following verses emphasize this matter and call on Muslims to respond to the Prophet of God, who invites them to what gives them a new life.

☐ Say (O Prophet), 'If you love God, then follow me; God will love you and forgive you your sins, and God is all-forgiving, all-merciful.'
Say, 'Obey God and the Apostle.' But if they turn away, indeed God does not like the faithless. (3:31-32)

☐ Whoever obeys the Apostle certainly obeys God; and as for those who turn their backs on you (O Prophet), We have not sent you to keep watch over them. (4:80)

☐ Whoever obeys God and the Apostle—they are with those whom God has blessed, including the prophets and the truthful, the martyrs and the righteous, and excellent companions are they! (4:69)

☐ But no, by your Lord! They will not believe until they make you (O Prophet) a judge in their disputes, then do not find within their hearts any dissent to your verdict and submit in full submission. (4:65)

☐ A faithful man or woman may not have any option in their matter when God and His Apostle have decided on a matter, and whoever disobeys God and His Apostle has certainly strayed into manifest error. (33:36)

☐ All the response of the faithful, when they are summoned to God and His Apostle that He may judge between them, is to say, 'We hear and obey.' It is they who will be felicitous. Whoever obeys God and His Apostle and fears God and is wary of Him—it is they who will be triumphant. (24:51-52)

☐ —Those who follow the Apostle, the untaught prophet, whose mention they find written with them in the Torah and the Gospel, who bids them to do what is right and forbids them from what is wrong, makes lawful to them all the good things and forbids them from all vicious things, and relieves them of their burdens and the shackles that were upon them—those who believe in him, honour him, and help him and follow the light that has been sent down with him,b they are the felicitous.' (7:157)

☐ The spoils that God gave to His Apostle from the people of the townships, are for God and the Apostle, the relatives and the orphans, the needy and the traveller, so that they do not circulate among the rich among you.

Take whatever the Apostle gives you, and refrain from whatever he forbids you, and be wary of God. God is indeed severe in retribution. (59:7)

☐ O you who have faith! Answer God and the Apostle when he summons you to that which will give you life. Know that God intervenes between a man and his heart and that you will be mustered toward Him. (8:24)

Spiritual Strengthening of the Prophet

The Apostle of God had a heavy task placed upon his shoulders. He should call people to something for which there was no precedent in their past history. Naturally, that would lead to opposition and hostility, and the Prophet must tolerate any hostility, oppression, and persecution of the opponents. It is clear that enduring all these hardships was not an easy task. That is why God, by strengthening his spirituality, raised the threshold of tolerance and patience and explained to him with all kinds of exhortations that his spirit should not be broken by untold hardships.

In the verses chosen for this topic, we see that God reassures His Prophet and exhorts him to have patience and reminds him of some of the special blessings He has given him.

☐ Whatever that We relate to you (O Prophet) of the accounts of the past apostles are those by which We strengthen your heart, and there has come to you in this *sūrah* the truth and an advice and admonition for the faithful. (11:120)

☐ We certainly know that what they say grieves you. Yet it is not you (O Prophet) that they deny, but it is God's signs that the wrongdoers impugn.
Apostles were certainly denied before you, yet they patiently bore being denied and tormented until Our help came to them.
Nothing can change the words of God, and there have certainly come to you (O Prophet) some of the accounts of the past apostles. (6:33-34)

☐ So (O Prophet) do not let their remarks grieve you. We indeed know whatever they hide and whatever they disclose. (36:76)

☐ So be patient! God's promise is indeed true. And do not let yourself (O Prophet) be upset by those who have no conviction. (30:60)

☐ So be patient, and you cannot be patient except with God's help. And do not grieve for them, nor be upset by their guile. Indeed, God is with those who are Godwary and those who are virtuous. (16:127-128)

☐ So submit patiently to the judgement of your Lord, for indeed you (O Prophet) fare before Our eyes. And celebrate the praise of your Lord when you rise at dawn, and also glorify

Him during the night and at the receding of the stars. (52:48-49)

⬜ Certainly We know that you become upset because of what they say. So celebrate the praise of your Lord and be among those who prostrate, (15:97-98)

⬜ Did We not open your breast for you (O Prophet) and relieve you of your burden which almost broke your back? Did We not exalt your name? (94:1-4)

⬜ By the morning brightness, and by the night when it is calm! Your Lord (O Prophet) has neither forsaken you, nor is He displeased with you, and the Hereafter shall be better for you than the world. Soon your Lord will give you that with which you will be pleased. (93:1-5)

⬜ We have indeed given you abundance. So pray to your Lord, and sacrifice the sacrificial camel. Indeed, it is your enemy who is without posterity. (108:1-3)

The Prophet is to be Treated with Honour

The people of pagan Arabia, who gradually converted to Islam, did not observe the necessary etiquette and respect when they came into the presence of the Prophet of God. They treated him according to their own ignorant culture. It was necessary to gradually teach them the polite manners to be observed in the presence of the Prophet.

In the selected verses, the etiquette of visiting the Prophet, attending his sessions, talking to him, questioning him, the necessity of obtaining his permission in certain matters and responding to his summons and other similar matters are stated.

⬜ O you who have faith! Do not venture ahead of God and His Apostle and be wary of God. God is indeed all-hearing, all-knowing. O you who have faith! Do not raise your voices above the voice of the Prophet, and do not speak aloud to him like you shout to one another, lest your works should fail without your being aware. Indeed, those who lower their voices in the presence of the Apostle of God—they are the ones whose hearts God has tested for Godwariness. For them will be forgiveness and a great reward.

Indeed, those who call you from behind the apartments, most of them do not use their reason. (49:1-4)

☐ O you who have faith! When you converse privately with the Apostle, offer a charity before your private talk. That is better for you and purer. But if you cannot afford to make the offering, then God is indeed all-forgiving, all-merciful.

Were you dismayed at having to offer charity before your private talks? Since you did not do it, and God has excused you for your failure to comply, now maintain the prayer and pay the zakāt, and obey God and His Apostle. God is well aware of what you do. (58:12-13)

☐ O you who have faith! Do not enter the Prophet's houses for a meal until you are granted permission, without waiting for it to be readied. But enter when you are invited, and disperse when you have taken your meal, without cozying up for chats. Such conduct on your part offends the Prophet, and he is ashamed of asking you to leave; but God is not ashamed of expressing the truth. When you ask his womenfolk for something, do ask them from behind a curtain. That is more chaste for your hearts and theirs. You should not offend the Apostle of God, nor may you ever marry his wives after him. That would indeed be a grave sin with God. (33:53)

☐ Indeed, the faithful are those who have faith in God and His Apostle, and when they are with him in a collective undertaking, they do not leave until they have sought his permission. They who seek your permission (O Prophet) are those who have faith in God and His Apostle. So when they seek your permission for some of their private work, give permission to whomever of them you wish and plead with God to forgive them. God is indeed all-forgiving, all-merciful. (24:62)

▢ O you who have faith! Do not ask about things which, if they are disclosed for you, will upset you. Yet if you ask about them while the Qur'an is being sent down, they shall be disclosed to you. God has excused it, and God is all-forgiving, all-forbearing. (5:101)

▢ Do not consider the Apostle's summons amongst you to be like your summoning one another. God certainly knows those of you who slip away, shielding one another from being noticed. Those who disobey his orders should beware lest an affliction should visit them or a painful punishment should befall them. (24:63)

▢ We did not send any apostle but to be obeyed by God's leave. Had they, when they wronged themselves, come to you (O Prophet) and pleaded to God for forgiveness, and the Apostle had pleaded forgiveness for them, they would have surely found God clement and merciful. (4:64)

Chapter 6

The Qur'an

The Greatness of the Qur'an

The Holy Qur'an is the sacred scripture of Islam, the eternal miracle of the Prophet and the panacea for all human mental and social ailments.

This blessed book, which is a brilliant light and a clear and compelling proof of the vital teachings of Islam, has been revealed to the Prophet during the 23 years of his mission and is a beacon of human life.

The Qur'an has not undergone any distortion and alteration, and remains as it had been revealed to the Prophet. It remains untouched by corruption and no false teaching has found way into it. It is a sacred document for humankind.

The Holy Qur'an has introduced itself in numerous verses, the following selected verses are a sample of the pertinent passages.

- This is indeed a noble Qur'an, in a guarded Book—no one touches it except the pure ones. (56:77-79)

- Indeed, We have sent down the Reminder, and, indeed, We will preserve it. (15:9)

The Qur'an

    ☐   It is indeed an august Book: falsehood cannot approach it, at present or in future, a revelation gradually sent down from One all-wise, all-laudable. (41:41-42)

    ☐   Blessed is this Book that We have sent down, confirming what was revealed before it, so that you (O Prophet) may warn the Mother of Cities (i.e., Mecca) and those around it. Those who believe in the Hereafter believe in it, and they are watchful of their prayers. (6:92)

    ☐   O mankind! Certainly a proof has come to you from your Lord, and We have sent down to you a manifest light. (4:174)

    ☐   This is a Book whose signs have been made definitive and then elaborated, from One who is all-wise, all-aware, (11:01)

    ☐   All praise belongs to God, who has sent down the Book to His servant and did not let any crookedness be in it, a Book upright, to warn of a severe punishment from Him, and to give good news to the faithful who do righteous deeds that there shall be for them a good reward, (18:1-2)

    ☐   I swear by what you see and what you do not see: it is indeed the speech of a noble apostle and it is not the speech of a poet. Little is the faith that you have!
Nor is it the speech of a soothsayer—little is the admonition that you take—gradually sent down from the Lord of all the nations. (69:38-43)

    ☐   Do not take the signs of God in derision, and remember God's blessing upon you, and what He has sent down to you of the Book and wisdom, to advise you therewith. Be wary of God, and know that God has knowledge of all things. (2:231)

    ☐   (O Prophet) We have sent down to you the Book with the truth, confirming what is before it of the scripture and as a guardian over it. So judge between them by what God has sent down, and do not follow their base desires against the truth that has come to you.

For each community among you We had appointed a code of law and a path, and had God wished He would have made you one community, but His purposes required that He should test you with respect to what He has given you.

So take the lead in all good works. To God shall be the return of you all, whereat He will inform you concerning that about which you used to differ. (5:48)

Revelation of the Qur'an

The Qur'an was revealed during the holy month of Ramadān and on the Night of Ordainment (*Laylat al-Qadr*), which is a blessed night that occurs every year. This book, as a blessed reminder of the Lord of the Worlds, was sent down through Gabriel, the Trustworthy Spirit, to the heart and soul of the Apostle of God to bring people out of darkness into the light.

- ☐ The month of Ramadān is one in which the Qur'an was sent down as guidance to mankind, with manifest proofs of guidance and the Criterion. (2:185)

- ☐ We sent it down on a blessed night and We have indeed been warning mankind. (94:3)

- ☐ Indeed, We sent it down on the Night of Ordainment. And what will show you what is the Night of Ordainment? The Night of Ordainment is better than a thousand months. (97:1-3)

- ☐ This is a Book We have sent down to you so that you (O Prophet) may bring mankind out from darkness into light, by the command of their Lord, to the path of the All-mighty, the All-laudable. (14:1)

- ☐ We sent them (i.e., the past prophets) with clear proofs and scriptures. We have sent down the Reminder to you so that you may clarify for these people that which has been sent down to them, so that they may reflect. (16:44)

☐ With the truth did We send it down, and with the truth did it descend, and We did not send you (O Prophet) except as a bearer of good news and warner. We have sent the Qur'an in discrete parts so that you may recite it for the people a little at a time, and We have sent it down piecemeal. (17:105-106)

☐ The gradual sending down of the Book is from God, the All-mighty, the All-wise. We have indeed sent down the Book to you with the truth; so worship God, putting exclusive faith in Him. (39:1-2)

☐ This too is a blessed reminder which We have sent down. Will you then deny it? (21:50)

☐ This is indeed a Book sent down by the Lord of all the nations, brought down by the Trustworthy Spirit upon your heart (so that you (O Prophet) may be one of the warners). (26:192-194)

☐ Thus have We sent down the Book to you; those to whom We have given the scripture (before) believe in it, and of these (Arabs) there are some who believe in it, and none contests Our signs except the faithless.

You (O Prophet) did not use to recite any scripture before it, nor did you write it with your right hand, for then the impugners would have been sceptical. Indeed, it is present as manifest signs in the breasts of those who have been given knowledge, and none contests Our signs except wrongdoers. (29:47-49)

☐ ... and it is not the speech of a poet. Little is the faith that you have! Nor is it the speech of a soothsayer—little is the admonition that you take—gradually sent down from the Lord of all the nations. (69:40-43)

Recitation of the Qur'an

The Holy Qur'an is at the height of sublimity both in respect of its lofty ideas, its rhetoric and literary excellence. Reciting the Qur'an and reading its words and expressions is rewarding in itself and illuminates the human heart even if one does not understand its meanings, because the reciter believes that what he is reading is the very word of God and divine revelation. Recitation of the Qur'an has its own prescribed etiquette partly mentioned in these verses.

☐ When you recite the Qur'an, seek the protection of God against the outcast Satan. (16:98)

☐ When the Qur'an is recited, listen to it and be silent, maybe you will receive God's mercy. (7:204)

☐ The faithless say, 'Why has not the Qur'an been sent down to him all at once?' So it was, that We may strengthen your heart with it, and We have recited it to you in a measured tone. (25:32)

☐ This is indeed a noble Qur'an, in a guarded Book —no one touches it except the pure ones— sent down gradually from the Lord of all the nations. (56:77-80)

☐ Indeed, those who recite the Book of God and maintain the prayer, and spend secretly and openly out of what We have provided them, expect a commerce that will never go bankrupt, so that He may pay them their full reward and enhance them out of His bounty. He is indeed all-forgiving, all-appreciative. (35:29-30)

☐ Recite what has been revealed to you from the Book of your Lord. Nothing can change His words, and you will never find any refuge besides Him. (18:27)

☐ Say (O Prophet), 'I have been commanded to worship

the Lord of this city (i.e., Mecca), who has made it inviolable and to whom all things belong, and I have been commanded to be among those who submit to God, and to recite the Qur'an.'

Whoever is guided is guided only for his own good, and as for him who goes astray, say, 'I am just one of the warners.' (27:91-92)

☐ Those to whom We have given the Book follow it as it ought to be followed: they have faith in it. As for those who deny it—it is they who are the losers. (2:121)

The Qur'an as Guidance

The Qur'an is a book of guidance, insight, and mercy, and it calls upon human beings to the most righteous and reliable way. It explains what is good and bad, beneficial and harmful for them, so that they may choose with thought and freedom.

The verses we have selected introduce the Qur'an as a scripture meant for human guidance and possessing various attributes. It is a source of light and a lamp in the darkness; it is an illuminating book, an exposition of things most essential for man to know, a vital source full of advice, mercy and insight; it is a revelation from the Creator, a herald of good news for the faithful and a panacea for sick humanity. These attributes are closely related to the attribute of guidance.

☐ This Qur'an indeed guides to what is most upright, and gives the good news to the faithful who do righteous deeds that there is a great reward for them. (17:9)

☐ O People of the Book! Certainly Our Apostle has come to you, clarifying for you much of what you used to hide of the Book, and excusing many an offense of yours. Certainly there has come to you a light from God and a manifest Book.

With it God guides those who pursue His pleasure to the ways of peace, and brings them out from darkness into light by His will, and guides them to a straight path. (5:15-16)

- This (Qur'an) is an explanation for mankind, and a guidance and advice for the Godwary. (3:138)

- When you (O Prophet) do not bring them a sign, they say, 'Why do you not improvise one?'
Say, 'I only follow what is revealed to me from my Lord; these are insights from your Lord, and guidance and mercy for people who have faith.' (7:203)

- We did not send down the Book to you (O Prophet) except for the purpose that you may clarify for them what they differ about, and as guidance and mercy for people who have faith. (16:64)

- The day We raise in every nation a witness against them from among themselves, We shall bring you (O Prophet) as a witness against these (Arabs). We have sent down the Book to you as a clarification of all things and as guidance, mercy and good news for those who submit to God. (16:89)

- O mankind! There has certainly come to you an advice from your Lord, and cure for what is in the breasts, and guidance and mercy for the faithful.
Say, 'In God's grace and His mercy—let them rejoice in that! It is better than what they amass.' (10:57-58)

- We send down in the Qur'an that which is a cure and mercy for the faithful, and it increases the wrongdoers only in loss. (17:82)

- Had We made it a non-Arabic Qur'an, they (i.e., the Arabs) would have said, 'Why have not its signs been articulated?' 'What! A non-Arabian scripture and an Arabian prophet!?'
Say, 'It is guidance and healing for those who have faith. As

for those who are faithless, there is a deafness in their ears and it is lost to their sight: to them it is as if they were being called from a far-off place.' (41:44)

◻   All praise belongs to God, who has sent down the Book to His servant and did not let any crookedness be in it, a Book upright, to warn of a severe punishment from Him, and to give good news to the faithful who do righteous deeds that there shall be for them a good reward. (18:01-02)

The Qur'an Confirms the Former Scriptures

The Qur'an, as the last divine book revealed to mankind, does not deny the earlier divine scriptures, but basically affirms their authenticity. The Qur'an itself represents a higher and ultimate stage in the history of divine revelation and is, in its own words, 'the guardian,' judge and arbiter over their contents, which resolves many theological controversies of preceding monotheistic traditions and clarifies many issues that have remained vague and ambiguous.

It is clear that the Qur'an is very different from other scriptures, but in principle it confirms their veracity and validity in their own time, because both the Qur'an and those books have been sent down from, or inspired by, the One God.

In the following selected verses, this issue has been emphasized in various ways, along with various other themes.

◻   Believe in that which I have sent down confirming that which is with you, and do not be the first ones to deny it, and do not sell My signs for a paltry gain, and be wary of Me alone.(2:41)

☐   Say, 'Whoever is an enemy of Gabriel should know that it is he who has brought it down on your heart with the will of God, confirming what has been revealed before it, and as a guidance and good news for the faithful.' (2:97)

☐   God—there is no god except Him—is the Living One, the All-sustainer. He has sent down to you the Book with the truth, confirming what was revealed before it, and He had sent down the Torah and the Gospel before as guidance for mankind, and He has sent down this Criterion. Indeed, there is a severe punishment for those who deny the signs of God, and God is all-mighty, avenger. (3:2-3)

☐   (O Prophet) We have sent down to you the Book with the truth, confirming what is before it of the Book and as a guardian over it. So judge between them by what God has sent down, and do not follow their base desires against the truth that has come to you.

For each community among you We had appointed a code of law and a path, and had God wished He would have made you all one community, but His purposes required that He should test you with respect to what He has given you.

So take the lead in all good works. To God shall be the return of you all, whereat He will inform you concerning that about which you used to differ. (5:48)

☐   That which We have revealed to you of the Book is the truth, confirming what was revealed before it. Indeed, God is aware and watchful of His servants.

Then We made those whom We chose from Our servants heirs to the scripture. Yet some of them are those who wrong themselves, and some of them are average, and some of them are those who take the lead in all the good works by God's will. That is the great grace of God! (35:31-32)

☐   And when there came to them an apostle from God,

confirming that which is with them, a part of those who were formerly given the scripture cast the Book of God behind their back, as if they did not know (that it is God's Book). (2:101)

☐ When there came to them (i.e., the Israelites residing in the Hijaz during the Prophet's times) a Book from God, confirming that which is with them—and earlier they would pray for victory over the pagans—so when there came to them what they recognized, they denied it. So may the curse of God be on the faithless! (2:89)

☐ This Qur'an could not have been fabricated by anyone besides God; rather, it is a confirmation of what was revealed before it, and an elaboration of the Book, there is no doubt in it, from the Lord of all the nations. (10:37)

☐ That which We have revealed to you of the Book is the truth, confirming what was revealed before it. Indeed, God is aware and watchful of His servants. (35:31)

☐ Blessed is this Book that We have sent down, confirming what was revealed before it, so that you may warn the Mother of Cities and those around it. Those who believe in the Hereafter believe in it, and they are watchful of their prayers. (6:92)

Comprehensiveness of the Qur'an

One of the most important characteristics of the Qur'an is its comprehensive and inclusive character, as it covers all things essential for human guidance. In its own words, it elaborates everything that is necessary for human felicity and salvation, which, of course, means everything that is needed to guide human beings.

The Qur'an has not omitted to say anything pertaining to human guidance and prosperity

☐ We have sent down the Book to you as a clarification

of all things and as guidance, mercy and good news for those who submit to God. (16:89)

☐ There is no animal on land nor bird that flies with its wings, but they are communities like yourselves. We have not omitted anything from the Book. Then they will be mustered toward their Lord. (6:38)

☐ Certainly We have variously paraphrased the principles of guidance in this Qur'an so that they may take admonition, but it increases them only in aversion. (17:41)

☐ Certainly we have drawn for mankind in this Qur'an every kind of parable. Indeed, if you bring them a sign, the faithless will surely say, 'You are nothing but fabricators!' (30:58)

☐ This Qur'an could not have been fabricated by anyone besides God; rather, it is a confirmation of what was revealed before it, and an elaboration of the Book, there is no doubt in it, from the Lord of all the nations.

Do they say, 'He has fabricated it?' Say, 'Then bring a *sūrah* like it, and invoke whomever you can, besides God, if you are truthful.' (10:37-38)

☐ This Qur'an is not a fabricated discourse; rather, it is a confirmation of what was revealed before it, and an elaboration of all things, and guidance and mercy for people who have faith. (12:111)

☐ Say, 'Shall I seek a judge other than God, while it is He who has sent down to you the Book whose contents have been well-elaborated?' Those We have given the Book know that it has been sent down from your Lord with the truth; so do not be one of the sceptics. (6:114)

Chapter 7

Communities and Groups

The Emergence of Communities & Role of the Prophets

an is a social being and human beings by their nature tend to live together. From the very beginning they have had a tendency to form communities and to serve one another to meet their needs. However, greed, envy and rivalry caused divisions and conflicts. So God sent the prophets to teach them to lead a peaceful and healthy communal life. Some of them were righteous and accepted the teachings of the prophets and some were not and went the way of Satan.

▢ Mankind were a single community; then God sent the prophets as bearers of good news and warners, and He sent down with them the Book with the truth, that it may judge between the people concerning that about which they differed, and none differed in it except those who were given it, after clear proofs had come to them, out of envy among themselves. Then God guided those who had faith to the truth of what they differed in, by His will, and God guides whomever He wishes to a straight path. (2:213)

▢ Mankind were but a single religious community; then they differed. And were it not for a prior decree of your Lord, decision would have been made between them concerning that about which they differ. (10:19)

☐ By God, We have certainly sent apostles to nations before you. But Satan made their deeds seem decorous to them. So he is their master today and there is a painful punishment for them. (16:63)

The Visage of the Faithful and the Faithless

In the Holy Qur'an, human beings are divided into two groups: the faithful and the righteous who obey God, and the faithless, who disbelieve and disobey God. Of course, each of these two groups, have their own subgroups.

In this division, the Qur'an lists in several verses the characteristics and attributes of each of these two groups and specifies their ultimate destiny. It also offers ways of greater advancement for the first group, as well as ways for the second of return to God.

The Faithful and the Godwary

In the verses we have chosen mention many attributes and signs of the faithful and the righteous. Some are related to belief and some to conduct. They have faith in God and the prophets and divine values, avoid evil and harmful deeds, perform their duties, and do not treat people unjustly.

☐ The faithful are only those whose hearts tremble with awe when God is mentioned, and when His signs are recited to them, they increase their faith, and who put their trust in their Lord, maintain the prayer and spend out of what We have provided them. It is they who are truly faithful. They shall have ranks near their Lord, forgiveness and a noble provision. (8:2-4)

☐ Certainly the faithful have attained salvation—those who are humble in their prayers, avoid vain talk, carry out their duty of *zakāt*, guard their private parts (except from their spouses or their slave women, for then they are not blameworthy; but whoever seeks anything beyond that—it is they who are transgressors), and those who keep their trusts and covenants and are watchful of their prayers. It is they who will be the inheritors, who shall inherit paradise and will remain in it [forever]. (23:1-11)

☐ They have faith in God and the Last Day, and bid what is right and forbid what is wrong, and they are active in performing good deeds. Those are among the righteous. Whatever good they do, they will not go unappreciated for it, and God knows well the Godwary. (3:114-115)

☐ The servants of the All-beneficent are those who walk humbly on the earth, and when the ignorant address them, say, 'Peace!' Those who spend the night for their Lord, prostrating and standing in worship. Those who say, 'Our Lord! Turn away from us the punishment of hell. Its punishment is indeed enduring. It is indeed an evil station and abode.' Those who are neither wasteful nor tight-fisted when spending, but balanced between these two extremes. Those who do not invoke another deity besides God, and do not kill a soul whose life God has made inviolable, except with due cause, and do not commit fornication. Whoever does that shall encounter its retribution, the punishment being doubled for him on the Day of Resurrection. (25:63-68)

☐ Those who do not give false testimony, and when they come upon frivolity, pass by with dignity. Those who, when reminded of the signs of their Lord, do not turn a deaf ear and a blind eye to them. And those who say, 'Our Lord! Give us joy and comfort in our spouses and offspring, and make us leaders of the Godwary.' (25:72-74)

☐ Hasten towards your Lord's forgiveness and a paradise as vast as the heavens and the earth, prepared for the Godwary—those who spend in ease and adversity, and suppress their anger, and excuse the faults of the people, and God loves the virtuous; and those who, when they commit an indecent act or wrong themselves, remember God, and plead to God seeking forgiveness for their sins—and who forgives sins except God?—and who knowingly do not persist in what sins they have committed. (3:133-135)

☐ O you who have faith! If you are wary of God, He will appoint a criterion for you, and absolve you of your misdeeds and forgive you, for God is dispenser of a mighty grace. (8:29)

☐ Is it not time yet for those who have faith that their hearts should be humbled for God's remembrance and toward the truth which has come down to them, not being like those who were given the Book before? Time took its toll on them and so their hearts were hardened, and many of them are transgressors. (57:16)

☐ Those who fulfil God's covenant and do not break the pledge solemnly made, and those who join what God has commanded to be joined, fear their Lord, and are afraid of an adverse reckoning—those who are patient for the sake of their Lord's pleasure, maintain the prayer, and spend secretly and openly out of what We have provided them, and repel others' evil conduct with good. For such will be the reward of the ultimate abode: (13:20-22)

☐ Only those shall maintain God's mosques who believe in God and the Last Day, and maintain the prayer and give the *zakāt*, and fear no one except God. They, hopefully, will be among the guided. (9:18)

☐ Those who have faith and whose hearts find rest in the

remembrance of God.' Behold! The hearts find rest solely in God's remembrance! (13:28-29)

☐ Those who have faith and do righteous deeds—happy are they and good is their ultimate destination.

All the response of the faithful, when they are summoned to God and His Apostle that He may judge between them, is to say, 'We hear and obey.' It is they who will be felicitous. Whoever obeys God and His Apostle and fears God and is wary of Him—it is they who will be triumphant. (24:51-52)

☐ But the faithful, men and women, are friends of one another: they bid what is right and forbid what is wrong and maintain the prayer, give the *zakāt*, and obey God and His Apostle. It is they to whom God will soon grant His mercy. God is indeed all-mighty, all-wise. (9:71)

☐ The faithful are indeed brothers. Therefore, make peace between your brothers and be wary of God, so that you may receive His mercy. (49:10)

The Faithless and the Evildoers

The second group, who are faithless, transgressors and oppressors, have attributes by which they are known and for which they are prevented from attaining felicity and suffer the punishment of God. They have false beliefs and do not believe in the religion of God. Some of them may have true beliefs but they disobey God and commit sins and violate the rights of others and oppress people.

In these verses some of their attributes are mentioned. Of course, there are other characteristics that are mentioned in other verses.

☐ Worldly life has been glamorized for the faithless, and they ridicule the faithful. But those who are Godwary shall be above them on the Day of Resurrection, and God provides for whomever He wishes without any reckoning. (2:212)

☐   We do not send the apostles except as bearers of good news and warners, but those who are faithless dispute fallaciously to refute thereby the truth, having taken in derision My signs and what they are warned of. (18:56)

☐   Those who deny the signs of God and the encounter with Him—they have despaired of My mercy, and for such there is a painful punishment. (29:23)

☐   When Our manifest signs are recited to them, you perceive denial on the faces of the faithless: they would almost pounce upon those who recite Our signs to them. Say, 'Shall I inform you about something worse than that? The Fire which God has promised the faithless, and it is an evil destination.' (22:72)

☐   Woe to every sinful liar, who hears the signs of God being recited to him, yet persists arrogantly as if he had not heard them. So inform him of a painful punishment. When he learns anything about Our signs, he takes them in derision. For such there is a humiliating punishment. (45:7-9)

☐   And do not obey any vile swearer, scandal-monger, talebearer, hinderer of all good, sinful transgressor, callous and, on top of that, base-born—who behaves thus only because he has wealth and children. When Our signs are recited to him, he says, 'Myths of the ancients!' Soon We shall brand him on his snout. (68:10-16)

☐   Say, 'Shall we inform you about the biggest losers in their works? Those whose efforts are misguided in the life of the world, while they suppose they are doing good.' (18:103-104)

☐   As for the faithless, their works are like a mirage in a plain, which the thirsty man supposes to be water. When he comes to it, he finds it to be nothing; but there he finds God, who will pay him his full account, and God is swift at reckoning. (24:39)

☐ Those who break the covenant made with God after having pledged it solemnly, and sever what God has commanded to be joined, and cause corruption on the earth—it is they who are the losers. (2:27)

☐ Do not be like those who forget God, so He makes them forget their own souls. It is they who are the transgressors. (59:19)

☐ Indeed, the faithless spend their wealth to bar from the way of God. Soon they will have spent it, then it will be a cause of regret to them, then they will be overcome, and the faithless will be gathered toward Hell, (8:36)

☐ For those who have committed misdeeds, the requital of a misdeed shall be its like, and they shall be overcast by abasement. They shall have no one to protect them from God. They will be as if their faces were covered with dark patches of the night. They shall be the inmates of the Fire, and they shall remain in it [forever]. (10:27)

☐ The hypocrites, men and women, are all alike: they bid what is wrong and forbid what is right, and are tight-fisted. They have forgotten God, so He has forgotten them. The hypocrites are indeed the transgressors. (9:67)

☐ And do not plead for those who betray themselves; indeed God does not like those who are treacherous and sinful. They try to hide their real character from people, but they do not try to hide from God, though He is with them when they conspire overnight with a discourse that He does not approve of. And God encompasses whatever they do. (4:107-108)

NON-MUSLIM COMMUNITIES

During the first decades of the Islamic era the Muslims had to deal with three major groups: the polytheists, the Jews and the Christians. The largest group was constituted by pagan Arab tribes who constituted the great majority of the Arabian population and were led by the Quraysh, the tribe of the Meccan oligarchs, who controlled the shrine at Mecca. The Quraysh had led the pagan troops against the Muslims, fighting three major battles against the nascent Muslim state until the treaty of Hudaybiyyah was signed in 6 AH/628 C.E.

Then there were the Jewish tribes, some of them living in the immediate neighbourhood of the Muslims in Medina and some based further north. Also, there were Christian settlements in the region of Najran to the south, whereas Palestine and Syria to the north were controlled by the Byzantine empire.

Most of the polemical rhetoric of the Qur'an is directed against the polytheists, many of whose practices including idolatry and infanticide are condemned in strong terms. The criticism of the Jews continues the tradition of the Hebrew prophets, and the majority of them are condemned for lack of faith, corruption and violation of the teachings of the Torah, and exploitative practices. The Qur'anic criticism of the Christians pertains mainly to their exorbitant doctrines relating to the trinity and divinity of Christ, but their majority is held guilt of violating divine commands.

☐ Say, 'We have faith in God and that which has been sent down to us, and that which was sent down to Abraham,

Ishmael, Isaac, Jacob and the Tribes, and that which Moses and Jesus were given, and what the prophets were given from their Lord; we make no distinction between any of them and to Him do we submit.' (2:136)

The Sole Criterion is Faith and Righteous Conduct

The Qur'an is explicit in several verses that the ultimate criterion for human salvation is faith and right conduct, irrespective of religious tradition and affiliation. Muslim theologians and exegetes often avoid the clear implications of such verses by reinterpreting them. However, they also acknowledge that everyone is answerable only to the extent that the divine teachings have reached him/her.

- By Time! The human being is indeed in loss, except those who have faith and do righteous deeds, and enjoin one another to follow the truth, and enjoin one another to patience [and fortitude]. (103:1-3)

- It will be neither after your hopes (O Muslims), nor the hopes of the People of the Book: whoever commits evil shall be requited for it, and he will not find for himself besides God any friend or helper. And whoever does righteous deeds, whether male or female, should he be faithful—such shall enter paradise and they will not be wronged [so much as] the speck on a date-stone. (4:123-124)

- Indeed, the faithful, the Jews, the Sabaeans, and the Christians—those who have faith in God and the Last Day and act righteously—they will have no fear, nor will they grieve. (2:62)

- For every nation We have appointed rites of worship which they observe; so let them not dispute with you about your religion. And invite to your Lord. You are indeed on a straight guidance. (22:67)

☐   We have sent down to you the Book with the truth, confirming what went before it of the scripture and as a guardian over it. So judge between them by what God has sent down, and do not follow their base desires against the truth that has come to you.

For each community among you We had appointed a code of law and a path, and had God wished He would have made you one community, but His purposes required that He should test you with respect to what He has given you.

So take the lead in all good works. To God shall be the return of you all, whereat He will inform you concerning that about which you used to differ. (5:48)

☐   Indeed, the faithless from among the People of the Book and the polytheists will be in the fire of hell, to remain in it. It is they who are the worst of creatures. (98:6)

Relations with Non-Muslims

The manner in which different classes of non-Muslims and aliens are to be treated in Islamic society has its own rules. Goodwill and good faith is advised towards them if they do not take steps harming Muslims. Muslims are permitted to share food with Christians and Jews as well as to marry women from those communities.

Freindly relations are envisaged with all non-Muslim communities. But if they plot and fight against Muslims, they must be dealt with from a position of power and there cannot be any friendly relations and alliances with them.

In the following verses, Muslims are told to have normal humane relations even with pagan and polytheist communities and they are forbidden from vilifying their idols. They are exhorted to refrain from violating treaties and agreements with other communities and nations unless first breached by the other side. In circumstances where relations with other communities are hostile, Muslims are urged to refrain from treating the enemy unjustly.

☐ God does not forbid you from dealing with kindness and justice with those polytheists who did not make war against you on account of religion and did not expel you from your homes. God indeed loves the just. God forbids you only in regard to those who made war against you on account of religion and expelled you from your homes and supported [the Makkans] in your expulsion, that you make friends with them, and whoever makes friends with them—it is they who are the wrongdoers. (60:8-9)

☐ Do not abuse those whom they invoke besides God, lest they should abuse God out of hostility, without any knowledge. That is how We have made their conduct seem decorous to every people. Then their return will be to their Lord and He will inform them concerning what they used to do. (6:108)

☐ If any of the polytheists seeks asylum from you (during a time of war), grant him asylum until he hears the Word of God. Then convey him to his place of safety. That is because they are a people who do not know. (9:6)

☐ Today all the good things have been made lawful for you—the food of those who were given the Book (e.i., Jews and Christians) is lawful for you, and your food is lawful for them—and chaste ones from among faithful women, and chaste women of those who were given the Book before you, when you have given them their dowries, in wedlock, not in license, nor taking paramours. (5:5)

☐ Do not argue with the People of the Book except in a manner which is best, except such of them as are wrongdoers, and say, 'We believe in what has been sent down to us and in what has been sent down to you; our God and your God is one and the same and to Him do we submit.' (29:46)

☐ O you who have faith! Be maintainers of justice, as witnesses for God's sake, and ill feeling for a people[1] should never lead you to be unfair. Be fair; that is nearer to Godwariness, and be wary of God. God is indeed well aware of what you do. (5:8)

☐ O you who have faith! Do not take your confidants from others than yourselves; they (i.e., those belonging to communities and groups hostile to Islam and Muslims) will spare nothing to ruin you. They are eager to see you in distress. Hatred has already shown itself from their mouths, and what their breasts hide within is yet worse. We have certainly made the signs clear for you, should you exercise your reason. (3:118)

The People of the Book: Jews and Christians

Jews and Christians are often lumped together in Qur'anic addresses and addressed jointly as a people who have scriptures and are often mentioned by the appellation 'People of the Book.'

☐ Indeed, the faithful, the Jews, the Sabaeans, and the Christians—those who have faith in God and the Last Day and act righteously—they will have no fear, nor will they grieve.

☐ Say, 'O People of the Book! You do not stand on anything until you observe the Torah and the Gospel and what has been sent down to you from your Lord.'

Surely many of them will be increased by what has been sent down to you from your Lord in rebellion and unfaith. So do not grieve for the faithless lot.

O People of the Book! Certainly Our Apostle has come to

---

[1] That is, ill-feeling arising from past conflicts and hostilities, as existed between the early Muslims and the polytheists of Mecca.

you, clarifying for you much of what you used to hide of the Book, and excusing many [an offense of yours]. Certainly there has come to you a light from God and a manifest Book. With it God guides those who pursue His pleasure to the ways of peace, and brings them out from darkness into light by His will, and guides them to a straight path. (5:15-16)

⬚ The Jews and the Christians say, 'We are God's children and His beloved ones.'

Say, 'Then why does He punish you for your sins?' No, you are humans from among His creatures. He forgives whomever He wishes and punishes whomever He wishes, and to God belongs the kingdom of the heavens and the earth and whatever is between them, and toward Him is your return.

O People of the Book! Certainly Our Apostle has come to you, clarifying [the Divine teachings] for you after a gap in [the appearance of] the apostles, lest you should say, 'There did not come to us any bearer of good news nor any warner.' Certainly there has come to you a bearer of good news and warner. And God has power over all things. (5:18-19)

⬚ They say, 'No one will enter paradise except one who is Jew or Christian.' Those are their false hopes! Say, 'Produce your evidence, should you be truthful.' Certainly whoever submits his will to God and is virtuous, he shall have his reward with his Lord, and they will have no fear, nor shall they grieve. (2:112)

⬚ Yet they are not all alike. Among the People of the Book is an upright nation; they recite God's signs in the watches of the night and prostrate. They have faith in God and the Last Day, and bid what is right and forbid what is wrong, and they are active in [performing] good deeds. Those are among the righteous. Whatever good they do, they will not go unappreciated for it, and God knows well the Godwary. (3:113-115)

⬚ Say, 'O People of the Book! Come to a common word

between us and you: that we will worship no one but God, that we will not ascribe any partner to Him, and that some of us will not take some others as lords besides God.' But if they turn away, say, 'Be witnesses that we have submitted to God.' (3:64)

☐ Say, 'O People of the Book! Why do you deny the signs of God, while God is witness to what you do?' Say, 'O People of the Book! why do you bar the faithful from the way of God, seeking to make it crooked, while you are witnesses to its truthfulness? And God is not oblivious of what you do.' (3:98-99)

☐ O you who have faith, if you obey a part of those who were given the Book, they will turn you back, after your faith, into faithless ones. And how would you be faithless while the signs of God are recited to you and His Apostle is in your midst? Whoever takes recourse in God is certainly guided to a straight path. (3:98-101)

Israelites/Jews

The call to *remember* is a memorable motif of the Hebrew Bible: "Remember that you were slaves in Egypt and that the Lord your God brought you out of there with a mighty hand and an outstretched arm."[1] The same call is often resounded in the Qur'an[2] and the Israelites are summoned to fulfil their side of the covenant, which is still regarded as valid and capable of fulfilment by the both sides. The Qur'anic criticism of the Israelites is severe and in line with the strong reproofs of the Hebrew scripture. While a group among them is commended for its faith and fairness, the majority are reprimanded for their lack of faith and past and current misconduct, including allying against the Muslims with the pagans and spying for them.

---

[1] Deuteronomy 5:15.
[2] 2:40, 47, 49, 122; 7:141; 14:6.

☐ O Children of Israel, remember My blessing which I bestowed upon you, and fulfil My covenant that I may fulfil your covenant, and be in awe of Me alone. And believe in that which I have sent down confirming that which is with you, and do not be the first ones to deny it, and do not sell My signs for a paltry gain, and be wary of Me alone. Do not mix the truth with falsehood, nor conceal the truth while you know. And maintain the prayer, and give the tithe, and bow down along with those who bow [in prayer]. (2:40-43)

☐ Among the people of Moses is a nation who guide [the people] by the truth and do justice thereby. (7:159)

☐ Certainly God took a pledge from the Children of Israel, and We raised among them twelve chiefs. And God said, 'I am with you! Surely, if you maintain the prayer and give the tithe and have faith in My apostles and support them and lend God a good loan, I will surely absolve you of your misdeeds, and I will surely admit you into gardens with streams running in them. But whoever of you disbelieves after that has certainly strayed from the right way.'

Then We cursed them because of their breaking their covenant and made their hearts hard: they pervert words from their meanings, and have forgotten a part of what they were reminded. You will not cease to learn of some of their treachery, excepting a few of them. Yet excuse them and forbear. Indeed, God loves the virtuous. (5:12-13)

☐ Certainly We took a pledge from the Children of Israel and We sent apostles to them. Whenever an apostle brought them that which was not to their liking, they would impugn a part of them and a part they would slay.

They supposed there would be no testing, so they became blind and deaf. Thereafter God accepted their repentance, yet again many of them became blind and deaf, and God watches what they do. (5:70-71)

☐ O Apostle! Do not grieve for those who are active in [promoting] unfaith, such as those who say, 'We believe' with their mouths, but whose hearts have no faith, and the Jews who eavesdrop with the aim of [telling] lies [against you] and eavesdrop for other people who do not come to you.

They pervert words from their meanings, [and] say, 'If you are given this, take it, but if you are not given this, beware!'

Yet whomever God wishes to mislead, you cannot avail him anything against God.

They are the ones whose hearts God did not desire to purify. There is disgrace for them in this world, and there is a great punishment for them in the Hereafter.

Eavesdroppers with the aim of [telling] lies, consumers of illicit gains! —if they come to you (O Prophet), judge between them, or disregard them. If you disregard them, they will not harm you in any way.

But if you do judge, judge between them with justice. Indeed, God loves the just.

And how should they make you a judge, while with them is the Torah, in which is God's judgement? Yet in spite of that they turn their backs [on Him] and they are not believers.

We sent down the Torah containing guidance and light. The prophets, who had submitted, judged by it for the Jews, and so did the rabbis and the scribes, as they were charged to preserve the Book of God and were witnesses to it…

In it We prescribed for them: a life for a life, an eye for an eye, a nose for a nose, and an ear for an ear, a tooth for a tooth, and retaliation for wounds. Yet whoever remits it out of charity, that shall be an atonement for him. (5:41-45)

☐ The faithless among the Children of Israel were cursed on the tongue of David and Jesus son of Mary. That, because they would disobey and commit transgressions. They would not forbid one another from the wrongs that they committed. Surely, evil is what they had been doing.

You see many of them allying with the faithless. Surely evil is what they have sent ahead for their own souls, as God is displeased with them and they shall remain in punishment [forever]. Had they believed in God and the Prophet and what has been sent down to him, they would not have taken them for allies. But most of them are transgressors. Surely, you will find the Jews and the polytheists to be the most hostile of all people towards the faithful. (5:78-82)

◌ We dispersed them into communities around the earth: some of them were righteous, and some of them otherwise, and We tested them with good and bad times so that they may come back. (7:168)

◌ Indeed, those who conceal what God has sent down of the Book and sell it for a paltry gain—they do not ingest into their bellies anything except fire, and God shall not speak to them on the Day of Resurrection, nor shall He purify them, and there is a painful punishment for them. They are the ones who bought error for guidance, and punishment for pardon: how patient of them to face the Fire! (2:174-175)

◌ Due to the wrongdoing of the Jews, We prohibited them certain good things that were permitted to them earlier, and for their barring many people from the way of God, and for their taking usury—though they had been forbidden from it—and for eating up the wealth of the people wrongfully. And We have prepared a painful punishment for the faithless among them.

But as for those who are firmly grounded in knowledge from among them and faithful, they believe in what has been sent down to you, and what was sent down before you those who maintain the prayer, give the tithe, and believe in God and the

Last Day—them We shall give a great reward. (4:160-162)

☐ O you who have faith! Do not take those who take your religion in derision and play, from among those who were given the Book before you, and the pagans, as allies, and be wary of God, should you be faithful.

When you call to prayer, they take it in derision and play. That is because they are a people who do not reason.

Say, 'O People of the Book! Are you vindictive toward us for any reason except that we have faith in God and in what has been sent down to us and in what was sent down before, and that most of you are transgressors?'

Say, 'Shall I inform you concerning something worse than that as requital from God? Those whom God has cursed and with whom He is wrathful, and turned some of whom into apes and swine, and worshippers of satanic entities! Such are in a worse situation and more astray from the right way.'

When they come to you (O Prophet), they say, 'We believe.' Certainly they enter with disbelief and leave with it, and God knows best what they have been concealing. You see many of them actively engaged in sin and aggression and consuming illicit gains. Surely, evil is what they have been doing.

Why do not the rabbis and the scribes forbid them from sinful speech and consuming illicit gains? Surely, evil is what they have been working.

The Jews say, 'God's hand is tied up.' Tied up be their hands, and cursed be they for what they say! No, His hands are wide open: He bestows as He wishes.

Surely many of them will be increased by what has been sent to you (O Prophet) from your Lord in rebellion and unfaith, and We have cast enmity and hatred amongst them until the Day of Resurrection.

Every time they ignite the flames of war, God puts them out. They seek to cause corruption on the earth, and God does not like the agents of corruption.

Had the People of the Book believed and been Godwary, We would have absolved them of their misdeeds and admitted them into gardens of bliss.

Had they observed the Torah and the Gospel, and what was sent down to them from their Lord, they would have drawn nourishment from above them and from beneath their feet.

There is an upright group among them, but what many of them do is evil. (5:57-66)

☐ A group of the People of the Book were eager to lead you (Muslims) astray; yet they lead no one astray except themselves, but they are not aware.

O People of the Book! Why do you deny God's signs while you testify [to their truth]? O People of the Book! Why do you mix the truth with falsehood, and conceal the truth while you know it? A group of the People of the Book say, 'Believe in what has been sent down to the (Muslim) faithful at the beginning of the day, and disbelieve at its end, so that they may turn back [from their religion].' (3:69-72)

☐ Among the People of the Book is he who, if you entrust him with a quintal, will repay it to you, and among them is he who, if you entrust him with a dinar, will not repay it to you unless you stand persistently over him. That is because they say, 'We have no obligation to the non-Jews.'

But they attribute lies to God, and they know it. Those who sell God's covenant and their oaths for a paltry gain, and on the Day of Resurrection God will not speak to them, nor will He so much as look at them, nor will He purify them, and there is a painful punishment for them. (3:75, 77)

Christians

The Qur'an affirms Jesus' virgin birth (19:16-22) and

his great miracles. While acknowledging the common conviction among Jews and Christians that Jesus died on the cross (4:157), the Qur'an denies the veracity of such a belief and, consequently, of his assumed resurrection. The Gospels also report that Jesus met and conversed with his disciples after his presumed death, which supports the reasonable conclusion that nothing untoward as depicted in the passion account had happened to him. But the Qur'an almost explicitly affirms his assumption (4:158) into heaven, like that of Enoch and Isaiah before him according to biblical accounts.[1] Despite the short duration of his ministry among Palestinian Jews that hardly came to the notice of contemporary witnesses and historians, he is celebrated as 'messiah' in the Qur'an in view of his role as the culmination of prophecy in the Judaic tradition and herald of the 'gospel' or good news of the advent of God's Greatest Apostle, with whose appearance the phenomenon of prophesy was staged on a scale never witnessed before or ever since.

☐ We followed them (i.e., the Hebrew prophets) with Jesus son of Mary to confirm that which was before him of the Torah, and We gave him the Gospel containing guidance and light, confirming what was before it of the Torah, and as guidance and advice for the Godwary.

Let the people of the Gospel judge by what God has sent down in it… We have sent down to you the Book with the truth, confirming what is before it of the scripture and as a guardian over it. So judge between them by what God has sent down, and do not follow their desires against the truth that has come to you. (5:46-48)

---

[1] The Qur'an is believed to be referring to the assumption of Enoch/Idrīs in vv. 19:56-57: "And mention in the Book Idrīs. He was indeed a truthful man and a prophet, and We raised him to an exalted station."

☐ Surely, you will find the most hostile of all people towards the faithful to be the Jews and the polytheists, and surely you will find the nearest of them in affection to the faithful to be those who say 'We are Christians.' That is because there are priests and monks among them, and because they are not arrogant.

When they hear what has been revealed to the Apostle, you see their eyes fill with tears because of the truth that they recognize.

They say, 'Our Lord, we believe; so write us down among the witnesses. Why should we not believe in God and the truth that has come to us, eager as we are that our Lord should admit us among the righteous people?'

So, for what they said, God requited them with gardens with streams running in them, to remain in them [forever], and that is the reward of the virtuous. (5:68-86)

☐ Also from those who say, 'We are Christians,' We took their pledge; but they forgot a part of what they were reminded. So We stirred up enmity and hatred among them until the Day of Resurrection, and God will soon inform them concerning what they had been doing. (5:14)

☐ They are certainly faithless who say, 'God is identical with Christ, son of Mary.'

Say, 'Who could avail anything against God had He wished to destroy Christ, son of Mary, and his mother, and everyone upon the earth?'

To God belongs the kingdom of the heavens and the earth, and whatever is between them. He creates whatever He wishes, and God has power over all things. (5:17)

☐ O People of the Book! Do not exceed the bounds in your religion, and do not attribute anything to God except the truth. Jesus Christ, son of Mary, was only an apostle of God, and His Word that He cast toward Mary and a spirit from Him.

So have faith in God and His apostles, and do not say, 'God is a trinity.' Relinquish such a creed! That is better for you. God is but the One God. He is far too immaculate to have any son. To Him belongs whatever is in the heavens and whatever is on the earth, and God suffices as trustee.

Christ would never disdain being a servant of God, nor would the angels brought near to Him. And whoever disdains His worship and is arrogant, He will gather them all toward Him. As for those who have faith and do righteous deeds, He will pay them in full their rewards, and He will enhance them out of His grace. But those who are disdainful and arrogant, He will punish them with a painful punishment, and they will not find besides God any friend or helper. (4:171-173)

☐ They are certainly faithless who say, 'God is identical with Christ, son of Mary.'

But Christ had said, 'O Children of Israel! Worship God, my Lord and your Lord. Indeed, whoever ascribes partners to God, God will forbid him [entry into] paradise, and his refuge will be the Fire, and the wrongdoers will not have any helpers.'

They are certainly faithless who say, 'God is the third [person] of a trinity,' while there is no god except the One God.

If they do not desist from what they say, there shall befall the faithless among them a painful punishment.

Will they not repent to God and plead to Him for forgiveness? Yet God is all-forgiving, all-merciful.

Christ, son of Mary, is but an apostle. Certainly [other] apostles have passed before him, and his mother was a truthful one.

Both of them would eat food. Look how We clarify the signs for them, and yet, look, how they go astray!

Say, 'Do you worship, besides God, what has no power to bring you any benefit or harm, while God—He is the All-hearing, the All-knowing?!'

Say, 'O People of the Book! Do not unduly exceed the bounds

in your religion and do not follow the myths of a people who went astray in the past and led many astray, and [themselves] strayed from the right path.' (5:72-77)

▢ And for their (i.e., of the Jews) faithlessness, and their uttering a monstrous calumny against Mary, and for their saying, 'We killed Jesus Christ, son of Mary, the apostle of God—though they did not kill him, nor crucify him, but so it was made to appear to them. Indeed, those who differ concerning him are in doubt about him: they do not have any knowledge of that beyond following conjectures, and certainly they did not kill him. Indeed, God raised him up toward Himself, and God is all-mighty, all-wise. (4:156-158)

▢ And when (on Judgement's Day) God will say, 'O Jesus son of Mary! Was it you who said to the people, "Take me and my mother for gods besides God"?'

He will say, 'Immaculate are You! It does not behoove me to say what I have no right to. Had I said it, You would certainly have known it: You know whatever is in my self, and I do not know what is in Your Self. Indeed, You know best all that is Unseen. I did not say to them [anything] except what You had commanded me [to say]: "Worship God, my Lord and your Lord." I was a witness to them so long as I was among them. But when You had taken me away, You Yourself were watchful over them, and You are witness to all things. If You punish them, they are indeed Your servants; but if You forgive them, You are indeed the All-mighty, the All-wise.'

God will say, 'This day truthfulness shall benefit the truthful. For them there will be gardens with streams running in them, to remain in them forever. (5:116-119)

Chapter 8

Eschatology
Resurrection & Afterlife

God's Ability to Raise the Dead

The extant Torah does not provide any clear-cut teaching regarding life after death, with the result that, at the dawn of the Christian era, one of the Jewish sects whose members administered the Temple as priests did not believe in resurrection. Contemporary Jews also differ in their beliefs regarding resurrection and afterlife. Christians have more developed notions of resurrection, judgement and afterlife, but there is a great diversity of views concerning every aspect of eschatology.

In contrast with the former scriptures, the Qur'an offers a much fuller and vivid picture of the world of the Hereafter. One of the tenets of Islam, common to all Muslims irrespective of their sectarian affiliation, is the belief in resurrection and it is mentioned in many verses of the Qur'an. At a certain time known only to God all human beings will be resurrected after death, burial, decay and return to the soil. The physical remnants of their bodies will be transformed into living bodies, and all human beings will be brought together into a vast realm, where they will be gathered together for judgement and rewarded or punished according to their deeds in the world.

The first stage of resurrection is the quickening of the dead, which seems very unlikely to those who do not believe in the absolute power of God. The polytheists of the age of the Prophet denied the possibility of resurrection and ridiculed the Apostle of God for asserting such a belief.

The following verses are related to this subject. They cite examples from this world itself, and emphasize that resurrection of the dead is not beyond God's infinite power. It is simple for Him to revive the dead.

▫ So observe the effects of God's mercy: how He revives the earth after its death! He is indeed the reviver of the dead and He has power over all things. (30:50)

▫ It is God who sends the winds and they raise a cloud; then We drive it toward a dead land and with it revive the earth after its death. Likewise will be the resurrection of the dead. (35:9)

▫ Among His signs is that you see the earth desolate; but when We send down water upon it, it stirs and swells. Indeed, He who revives it will also revive the dead. Indeed, He has power over all things. (41:39)

▫ Man draws comparisons for Us, and forgets his own creation. He says, 'Who will revive the bones when they have decayed?'
Say, 'He will revive them who produced them the first time, and He has knowledge of all creation. He, who made for you fire out of the green tree, and behold, you light fire from it! Is not He who created the heavens and the earth able to create the like of them? Yes indeed! He is the All-creator, the All-knowing. (36:78-81)

☐ Do they not see that God, who created the heavens and the earth and who was not exhausted by their creation, is able to revive the dead? Yes, indeed He has power over all things. (46:33)

The Day of Resurrection

The resurrection will take place at a time known only to God. It will be accompanied with catastrophic changes in the world. Some of these changes will occur on the eve of the resurrection, and some will occur after that.

These verses foretell that great event, when every human being will be judged on the basis of the record of his/her deeds in the world, and God will inform him of all that he has done.

☐ The people question you (O Prophet) concerning the Hour. Say, 'Its knowledge is only with God.' What do you know, maybe the Hour is near. (33:63)

☐ When the Imminent Hour befalls —there is no denying that it will befall—it will be lowering and exalting. (56:1-3)

☐ Be on the alert for the day when the caller will call from a close quarter, the day when they hear the Cry in all truth. That is the day of rising from the dead.
It is indeed We who give life and bring death, and toward Us is the final destination. The day the earth is split open for exhuming them, they will come out hastening. That mustering is easy for Us to carry out. (50:41-44)

☐ The day when the sky with its clouds will be split open and the angels will be sent down in a majestic descent, on that day true sovereignty will belong to the All-beneficent, and it will be a hard day for the faithless.
It will be a day when the wrongdoer will bite his hands,

saying, 'I wish I had followed the Apostle's way! Woe to me! I wish I had not taken so and so as a friend! (25:25-28)

☐ I swear by the Day of Resurrection! And I swear by the self-critical soul! Does man suppose that We will not put together his bones at resurrection? Of course, We are able to reshape even his fingertips (with exactly the same fingerprints)!

Man indeed desires to go on living viciously. He asks, 'When will this "day of resurrection" be?!' But when the eyes are dazzled, the moon is eclipsed, and the sun and the moon are brought together, that day man will say, 'Where is the escape from this day?'

No indeed! There will be no refuge!

That day the final goal will be toward your Lord. That day man will be informed about what works he had sent ahead to the scene of judgement and the legacy that he had left behind. Rather, man is witness to his own self, though he should offer excuses to justify his faults. (75:1-15)

The Gathering of People at the Resurrection

On the Day of Resurrection, which will occur after a heavenly cry, all people will be present before God without exception. That day is the Day of Judgment and Retribution, and everyone will be requited according to his deeds and no one will be wronged or treated unjustly

☐ God—there is no god except Him—will surely gather you on the Day of Resurrection, in which there is no doubt; and who is more truthful in speech than God? (4:87)

☐ Say, 'The former and latter generations will indeed be gathered for the tryst of a known day. (56:49-50)

☐ 'This is the Day of Judgement. We have brought you together with the former peoples. (77:38)

☐ It will be but a single Cry, and behold, they will all be presented before Us! 'Today no soul will be wronged in the least, nor will you be requited except for what you used to do.' (36:53-54)

☐ Say, 'It is God who gives you life, then He makes you die. Then He will gather you on the Day of Resurrection, in which there is no doubt. But most people do not know.' (45:26)

People's State at Resurrection

The good and bad deeds of individual humans will take an incarnated 'bodily form' on the Day of Resurrection, and people will encounter them with amazement, feeling regret for the shortcomings they had committed. That day the angels will hang the record of one's deeds around one's neck and he will be told to read it and be his own auditor and judge. On that day there will be bright faces and dark faces. The faithless with dark faces will suffer chastisement and the faithful with bright faces will be surrounded by God's mercy.

☐ The day when every soul will find present whatever good it has done; and as for the evil it has done, it will wish there were a far distance between it and itself. God warns you to beware of disobeying Him, and God is most kind to His servants. (3:30)

☐ The day when neither wealth nor children will avail, except him who comes to God with a sound heart, and paradise will be brought near for the Godwary, and hell will be brought into view for the perverse, (26:88-91)

☐ They are certainly losers who deny the encounter with God. When the Hour overtakes them suddenly, they will say, 'Alas for us, for what we neglected in it!' And they will bear their burdens on their backs. Behold, evil is what they bear! (6:31)

☐   We have strapped every person's karma to his neck, and We shall bring it out for him on the Day of Resurrection as a book that he will find wide open. 'Read your book! Today your soul suffices as your own reckoner.' (17:13-14)

☐   The day when they will emerge from their graves, nothing about them will be hidden from God. 'To whom does the sovereignty belong today?' 'To God, the One, the All-paramount!' 'Today every soul shall be requited for what it has earned. There will be no injustice today. God is indeed swift at reckoning.'

Warn them of the Approaching Day when the hearts will be at the throats, choking with suppressed agony, and the wrongdoers will have no sympathizer, nor any intercessor who might be heard. (40:16-18)

☐   On the day when some faces will turn white and some faces will turn black. As for those whose faces turn black, they will be told, 'Did you disbelieve after your faith? So taste the punishment because of what you used to disbelieve.' But as for those whose faces become white, they shall dwell in God's mercy, and they will remain in it [forever]. (3:106-107)

Doomsday Terror

The Day of Resurrection is the day of great terror, the day of a great earthquake in which nursing mothers will abandon their infants and pregnant women will deliver their burden and the people will be stupefied and befuddled though they will not be drunk. At the doomsday earthquake, the earth will brings forth its secrets, and people will ask, "What's going on?" They will receive the reply that the earth is responding to its Lord's command. That day will be so terrible that one will even seek to avoid one's closest relatives and flee one's brother and parents, spouse and children.

☐ O mankind! Be wary of your Lord! The quake of the Hour is indeed a terrible thing. The day that you will see it, every suckling female will be unmindful of what she suckled, and every pregnant female will deliver her burden, and you will see the people drunk, yet they will not be drunken, but God's punishment is severe. (22:1-2)

☐ When the earth is rocked with a terrible quake and discharges her burdens, and man says, 'What is the matter with her?' On that day she will relate her chronicles for her Lord will have inspired her.
On that day, mankind will issue forth in various groups to be shown their deeds. So whoever does an atom's weight of good will see it, and whoever does an atom's weight of evil will see it. (99:1-8)

☐ So when the deafening Cry comes— the day when a man will evade his brother, his mother and his father, his spouse and his sons— each of them will have a task to keep him preoccupied on that day. Some faces will be bright on that day, laughing and joyous, and some faces on that day will be covered with dust, overcast with gloom. It is they who are the faithless, the vicious (80:33-42)

☐ Woe to the deniers on that day —those who play around in vain talk, the day when they will be shoved forcibly toward the fire of hell and told: 'This is the Fire which you used to deny! Is this, then, also magic, or is it you who do not perceive? Enter it, and it will be the same for you whether you are patient or impatient. You are only being requited for what you used to do.' (52:11-16)

Fair Rewards and Punishments

On the Day of Retribution, which is the Day of Judgment, all good or bad deeds committed by human beings in the world will be reckoned precisely and will be rewarded or punished accordingly. Everyone will see the result of his actions. In this audit, no one will be done the slightest injustice and every action will be taken into account, though it should be as small as an atom or as little as a mustard seed.

All actions of an individual will handed over to him/her, written in a record, and he will be amazed to see how his every deed, small and great, has been recorded, and nothing has been left out.

> We shall set up just scales on the Day of Resurrection, and no soul will be wronged in the least. Even if it be the weight of a mustard seed We will produce it and We suffice as reckoners. (21:47)

> Beware of a day in which you will be brought back to God. Then every soul shall be recompensed fully for what it has earned, and they will not be wronged. (2:281)

> The day when every soul will find present whatever good it has done; and as for the evil it has done, it will wish there were a far distance between it and itself. God warns you to beware of disobeying Him, and God is most kind to His servants. (3:30)

> The Book will be set up. Then you will see the guilty apprehensive of what is in it. They will say, 'Woe to us! What a book is this! It omits nothing, big or small, without enumerating it.' They will find present whatever they had done, and your Lord does not wrong anyone. (18:49)

☐ But how will it be with them when We gather them on a day in which there is no doubt, and every soul shall be recompensed fully for what it has earned, and they will not be wronged? (3:25)

☐ 'Today every soul shall be requited for what it has earned. There will be no injustice today. God is indeed swift at reckoning.'

Warn them of the Approaching Day when the hearts will be at the throats, choking with suppressed agony, and the wrongdoers will have no sympathizer, nor any intercessor who might be heard. (40:17-18)

☐ And you will see every nation fallen on its knees. Every nation will be summoned to its book: 'Today you will be requited for what you used to do. This is Our book which speaks truly against you. Indeed, We used to record what you used to do.'

As for those who have faith and do righteous deeds, their Lord will admit them into His mercy. That is a manifest triumph! But as for the faithless, they will be asked, 'Were not My signs recited to you? But you were disdainful and you were a guilty lot. (45:28-31)

☐ The day We shall summon every group of people along with their leader (imam), then whoever is given his book in his right hand—they will read their book, and they will not be wronged so much as a single date-thread. (17:71)

☐ On that day, mankind will issue forth in various groups to be shown their deeds. So whoever does an atom's weight of good will see it, and whoever does an atom's weight of evil will see it. (99:7-8)

☐ The earth will glow with the light of her Lord and the Book will be set up, and the prophets and the martyrs will be brought, and judgment will be made between them with justice and they will not be wronged. Every soul will be recompensed fully for what it has done, and He is best aware of what they do. (39:69-70)

☐ For everyone there are degrees of merit pertaining to what they have done, so that He may recompense them fully for their works and they are be wronged. (46:19)

The Inhabitants of Paradise

The Qur'an presents such a detailed and vivid picture of paradise and hell that it is unmatched by any other scripture. Those who live with faith and act righteously, being wary of God, God will admit them at resurrection into an eternal paradise, as vast as the heaven and the earth, where they will receive all kinds of blessings. In paradise, besides enjoying all kinds of blessings, foods and drinks and other pleasures, they will also receive the higher and superior blessing, the approval and pleasure of their Creator, the ultimate achievement.

The verses chosen here describe all sorts of God's blessings for the inhabitants of paradise, which will be without end.

☐ Take the lead towards forgiveness from your Lord and a paradise as vast as the heavens and the earth, prepared for those who have faith in God and His apostles. That is God's grace, which He grants to whomever He wishes, and God is dispenser of a mighty grace. (57:21)

☐ God has promised the faithful, men and women, gardens with streams running in them, to remain in them forever, and good dwellings in the Gardens of Eden. Yet God's pleasure is greater than all these; that is the great success. (9:72)

☐ But as for him who is awed to stand before his Lord

and restrains his soul from following base desires, his refuge will indeed be paradise. (79:40-41)

☐ As for those who have faith and do righteous deeds— We task no soul except according to its capacity—they shall be the inhabitants of paradise and they shall remain in it forever. We will remove whatever rancour there is in their breasts, and streams will run for them.

They will say, 'All praise belongs to God, who guided us to this. Had not God guided us, we would have never been guided. Our Lord's apostles had certainly brought the truth.' The call will be made to them: 'This is paradise, which you have been given to inherit because of what you used to do!' (7:42-43)

☐ Gardens of Eden promised by the All-beneficent to His servants, while they were still unseen. His promise is indeed bound to come to pass. Therein they will not hear vain talk, but only 'Peace!' Therein they will have their provision morning and evening. This is the paradise that We will give as inheritance to those of Our servants who are Godwary. (19:61-63)

☐ Gardens of Eden, which they will enter, adorned therein with bracelets of gold and pearl, and their garments therein will be of silk. They will say, 'All praise belongs to God, who has removed all grief from us. Our Lord is indeed all-forgiving, all-appreciative, who has settled us in the everlasting abode by His grace. In it we are untouched by toil and untouched by fatigue.' (35:33-35)

☐ Those who believed in Our signs and had been submitting to God. (They shall be told:) 'Enter paradise, you and your spouses, rejoicing.' They will be served around with golden dishes and goblets, and therein will be whatever the souls desire and eyes delight in. 'You will remain in it. That is the paradise you have been given to inherit for what you used to do. There are abundant fruits for you in it from which you will eat.' (43:69-73)

☐ Those who are virtuous shall receive the best reward and an enhancement. Neither dust nor abasement shall overcast their faces. They shall be the inhabitants of paradise, and they shall remain in it forever. (10:26)

☐ But to those who were Godwary it will be said, 'What is it that your Lord has sent down?' They will say, 'Good.' For those who do good in this world there will be a good reward, and the abode of the Hereafter is better, and the abode of the Godwary is surely excellent: the Gardens of Eden, which they will enter, with streams running in them. There they will have whatever they wish, and thus does God reward the Godwary —those whom the angels take away while they are pure. They say to them, 'Peace be to you! Enter paradise because of what you used to do.' (16:30-32)

☐ Those who have faith and do righteous deeds, We will settle them in the lofty abodes of paradise, with streams running in them, to remain in them. How excellent is the reward of the workers! —Those who are patient and who put their trust in their Lord. (29:58-59)

☐ Those who are wary of their Lord will be led to paradise in throngs. When they reach it and its gates are opened, its keepers will say to them, 'Peace be to you! You are welcome! Enter it to remain.'
They will answer, 'All praise belongs to God, who has fulfilled His promise to us and made us inheritors of the earth, that we may settle in paradise wherever we may wish!' How excellent is the reward of the workers of righteousness! (39:73-74)

☐ And paradise will be brought near for the Godwary, it will not be distant any more: 'This is what you were promised. It is for every penitent and dutiful servant who fears the All-beneficent in secret and comes with a penitent heart. Enter it in peace! This is the day of immortality.' There they will have whatever they wish, and with Us there is yet more. (50:31-35)

☐ The pious will be amid bliss, observing as they recline on couches. You will perceive in their faces the freshness of bliss. They will be served with a sealed pure wine, whose seal is musk—for such let the viers vie— and whose seasoning is from *Tasnīm*, a spring where those brought near to God drink. (83:22-28)

The Inmates of Hell

As against the inhabitants of Paradise are the inmates of Hell, and they are the faithless ones who disbelieved and disobeyed God and insisted on their disbelief. They will suffer divine retribution at resurrection. They will seek the help of the angels of Hell, but help will be withheld from them. They will be very regretful in hell for what they have done in the world, but it will not benefit them.

☐ Say (O Prophet), 'Shall we inform you about the biggest losers in their works? Those whose efforts are misguided in the life of the world, while they suppose they are doing good.' They are the ones who deny the signs of their Lord and encounter with Him. So their works have failed. On the Day of Resurrection We will not give them any weight. That is their requital—hell—because of their unfaith and their deriding My signs and My apostles. (18:103-106)

☐ The faithless will be driven to hell in throngs. When they reach it and its gates are opened, its keepers will say to them, 'Did there not come to you any apostles from among yourselves, reciting to you the signs of your Lord and warning you of the encounter of this day of yours?' They will say, 'Yes, but the word of punishment became due against the faithless.' It will be said, 'Enter the gates of hell to remain in it. Evil is the ultimate abode of the arrogant.' (39:71-72)

☐ For those who defy their Lord is the punishment of hell, and it is an evil destination. When they are thrown in it they hear it blaring, as it seethes, almost exploding with rage. Whenever a group is thrown in it, its keepers will ask them, 'Did not any warner come to you?' They will say, 'Yes, a warner did come to us, but we impugned him and said, 'God did not send down anything; you are only in great error.' They will say, 'Had we listened or exercised our reason, we would not have been among inmates of the Blaze.' Thus they will admit their sin. So away with the inmates of the Blaze! (67:06-11)

☐ The day when the excuses of the wrongdoers will not benefit them, the curse will lie on them, and for them will be the ills of the ultimate abode. (40:52)

☐ As for the faithless, there is for them the fire of hell: they will neither be done away with so that they may die, nor shall its punishment be lightened for them. Thus do We requite every ingrate. They will cry therein for help: 'Our Lord! Bring us out, so that we may act righteously—differently from what we used to do!' {They shall be told:) 'Did We not give you a life long enough that one who is heedful might take admonition? And, moreover, the warner had also come to you. Now taste the consequence of your deeds, for the wrongdoers have no helper.' (35:36-37)

☐ (O Prophet) tell them, 'This is the truth from your Lord: let anyone who wishes believe it, and let anyone who wishes disbelieve it.'

We have indeed prepared for the wrongdoers a Fire whose curtains will surround them on all sides. If they cry out for help, they will be helped with a water like molten copper which will scald their faces. What an evil drink and how ill a resting place! (18:29)

☐ Indeed, We shall soon make those who deny Our signs

enter a Fire: as often as their skins become scorched, We shall replace them with other skins, so that they may taste the punishment. God is indeed all-mighty, all-wise. (4:56)

☐ They (i.e., the inhabitants of paradise) will be in gardens, questioning the guilty: 'What drew you into Hell?' They will answer, 'We were not among those who prayed. Nor did we feed the poor. We used to indulge in profane gossip along with the gossipers, and we used to deny the Day of Retribution until death came to us.' (74:40-47)

PART TWO

The Ethics of the Qur'an

Chapter 9

Values and Norms Individual and Social

Faith and Righteous Conduct

Human development has two aspects: material and spiritual. Spiritual development and edification are the result of faith and righteous conduct. Faith and works are inseparable. Real faith always manifests itself in one's behaviour. One who practices righteousness under the inspiration of faith attains a pure life in the world and enters Paradise in the Hereafter. God does not waste the reward of anyone who has done good work. Faith brings peace and calm to the soul and reassures the heart, and good deeds please God and bring great rewards.

☐ By Time! The human being is indeed in loss, except those who have faith and do righteous deeds, and enjoin one another to follow the truth, and enjoin one another to patience [and fortitude]. (103:1-3)

☐ Whoever acts righteously, whether male or female, should he be faithful, We shall revive him with a good life and pay them their reward by the best of what they used to do. (16:97)

☐ Whoever does righteous deeds, whether male or female, should he be faithful—such shall enter paradise and they will not be wronged so much as the speck on a date-stone. (4:124)

☐ As for those who have faith and do righteous deeds, He will pay them in full their rewards, and He will enhance them out of His grace. But those who are disdainful and arrogant, He will punish them with a painful punishment, and they will not find besides God any friend or helper. (4:173)

☐ As for those who have faith and do righteous deeds—indeed We do not waste the reward of those who are good in deeds. (18:30)

☐ God has promised those who have faith and do righteous deeds forgiveness and a great reward. As for those who are faithless and deny Our signs, they shall be the inmates of hell. (5:9)

☐ Indeed, those who have faith and do righteous deeds and are humble before their Lord—they shall be the inhabitants of paradise, and they shall remain in it [forever]. (11:23)

☐ Those who have faith and whose hearts find rest in the remembrance of God. Behold! The hearts find rest solely in God's remembrance!   Those who have faith and do righteous deeds—happy are they and good is their ultimate destination. (13:28-29)

☐ This Qur'an indeed guides to what is most upright, and gives the good news to the faithful who do righteous deeds that there is a great reward for them. (17:9)

☐ Indeed, those who have faith and do righteous deeds—the All-beneficent will endear them to His creation. (19:96)

☐ Whoever is faithful and does righteous deeds, his endeavour shall not go unappreciated, and We will indeed record it for him. (21:94)

☐ Indeed, those who have faith and do righteous deeds—it is they who are the best of creatures. Their reward, near their Lord, is the Gardens of Eden, with streams running in them, to remain in them forever. God is pleased with them, and they are pleased with Him. That is for those who fear their Lord. (98:7-8)

☐ Who has a better call than him who summons to God and acts righteously and says, 'I am indeed one of those who have submitted (to God)'? (41:33)

☐ Whoever seeks honour should know that honour entirely belongs to God. To Him ascends the good word, and He elevates righteous conduct; as for those who devise evil schemes, there is a severe punishment (35:10)

Knowledge, Awareness and Thought

The knowledge and awareness that come from thought and reflection are the most important means of human deliverance and felicity. They make persons humble towards the truth, prompt them to abandon injurious customs and beliefs and make new beginnings by exploring the realm of being and natural phenomena, providing release from false presuppositions. In many verses, some examples of which are cited here, the Holy Qur'an invites human beings to thought and reasoning. It grants an elevated status to persons of thought and wisdom and considers them to be the real servants of God.

☐ Indeed, in the creation of the heavens and the earth and the alternation of night and day, there are signs for those who possess intellect. Those who remember God standing, sitting, and lying on their sides, and reflect on the creation of the heavens and the earth and say, 'Our Lord, You have not created this in vain! Immaculate are You! Save us from the punishment of the

Fire. (3:190-191)

☐ Those who have been given knowledge see that what has been sent down to you (O Prophet) from your Lord is the truth and that it guides to the path of the All-mighty, the All-laudable. (34:6)

☐ Indeed, it is present as manifest signs in the breasts of those who have been given knowledge, and no one contests Our signs except wrongdoers. (29:49)

☐ Is he who supplicates in the watches of the night, prostrating and standing, being apprehensive of the Hereafter and expecting the mercy of his Lord … ? Say, 'Are those who know equal to those who do not know?' Only those who possess intellect take admonition. (39:9)

☐ Only those of God's servants having knowledge fear Him. God is indeed all-mighty, all-forgiving.
Indeed, those who recite the Book of God and maintain the prayer, and spend secretly and openly out of what We have provided them, expect a commerce that will never go bankrupt, so that He may pay them their full reward and enhance them out of His bounty. He is indeed all-forgiving, all-appreciative. (35:28-30)

☐ God—maintainer of justice, the Almighty and the All-wise, besides whom there is no god—bears witness that there is no god except Him, and so do the angels and those who possess knowledge. (3:18)

☐ We draw these parables for mankind; but no one grasps them except those who have knowledge. God created the heavens and the earth with consummate wisdom. There is indeed a sign in that for the faithful. (29:43-44)

☐ Those who were given knowledge said to them (i.e., those who envied Korah for his riches), 'Woe to you! God's reward is better for someone who has faith and acts righteously, and no one will receive it except the patient.' (28:80)

☐ (O Prophet) We did not send any apostles before you except as humans to whom We revealed. Ask the People of the Reminder if you do not know. We sent them with clear proofs and scriptures. We have sent down the Reminder to you so that you may clarify for these people that which has been sent down to them, so that they may reflect. (16:43-44)

☐ It is He who has spread out the earth and set in it firm mountains and streams, and of every fruit He has made in it two kinds. He draws the night's cover over the day. There are indeed signs in that for people who reflect. (13:3)

☐ Know that God revives the earth after its death. We have certainly made the signs clear for you, so that you may exercise your reason. (57:17)

☐ He disposed the night and the day for you, and the sun, the moon and the stars are disposed by His command. There are indeed signs in that for people who exercise their reason.
And He disposed for your benefit whatever He has created for you in the earth of diverse hues—there is indeed a sign in that for people who take admonition. (16:12-13)

Repentance From Sin

Those who believe in God and His Prophet must always be careful of their deeds and refrain from disobeying God, and if they have committed a sin, they must repent immediately, regretting their misdeed and not repeat it. Then God will forgive them by accepting their repentance.

Repentance works if one repents in the normal course of life, but if one puts it of until the very verge of death and repents while dying, the repentance is not accepted.

☐ O you who have faith! Repent to God with sincere repentance! Maybe your Lord will absolve you of your misdeeds and admit you into gardens with streams running in them, on the day when God will not let down the Prophet and the faithful who are with him. Their light will move swiftly before them and on their right. They will say, 'Our Lord! Perfect our light for us and forgive us! Indeed, You have power over all things.' (66:8)

☐ Acceptance of repentance by God is only for those who commit evil out of ignorance and then repent promptly. It is such whose repentance God will accept, and God is all-knowing, all-wise. But acceptance of repentance is not for those who go on committing misdeeds: when death approaches any of them, he says, 'I repent now.' Nor is it for those who die while they are faithless. For such We have prepared a painful punishment. (4:17-18)

☐ We do not send the apostles except as bearers of good news and warners. As for those who are faithful and righteous, they will have no fear, nor will they grieve. (6:54)

☐ Indeed, the hypocrites will be in the lowest reach of the Fire, and you will never find any helper for them, except for those who repent and reform and hold fast to God and dedicate their religion exclusively to God. Those are with the faithful, and soon God will give the faithful a great reward. (4:145-146)

☐ Yet to those who commit misdeeds, but repent after that and believe—indeed, after that, your Lord shall surely be all-forgiving, all-merciful. (7:153)

☐ It is He who accepts the repentance of His servants and excuses their misdeeds and knows what you do. He answers the supplications of those who have faith and do righteous deeds and enhances them out of His grace. But as for the faithless, there is a severe punishment for them. (42:25-26)

☐ 'O my people! Plead with your Lord for forgiveness, then turn to Him penitently: He will send copious rains for you from the sky, and add power to your present power. So do not turn your backs on Him as guilty ones.' (11:52)

☐ Plead with your Lord for forgiveness, then turn to Him penitently. He will provide you with a good provision for a specified term and grant His grace to every meritorious person. But if you turn your backs on Him, indeed I fear for you the punishment of a terrible day. (11:3)

The Invitation to Virtues

The basic concern of Islam is to provide human beings well-being and felicity in this life and the Hereafter. Therefore, it calls on human beings to espouse values and duties that ensure this goal. One of them is to invite people to do good and avoid harmful behaviour. When one invites others to do good, one is naturally further drawn toward the same goals. The general invitation to bid what is right and forbid what is wrong and injurious and making it a public duty to call for observation of ethical values and healthy social norms serves to institutionalize these values and norms.

☐ There has to be a nation among you summoning to the good, bidding what is right, and forbidding what is wrong. It is they who are the felicitous. (3:104)

☐ Who has a better call than him who summons to God and acts righteously and says, 'I am indeed one of those who have submitted to God (muslims)'? (41:33)

☐ (O Prophet,) invite to the way of your Lord with wisdom and good advice and dispute with them in a manner that is best. Indeed, your Lord knows best those who stray from His way, and He knows best those who are guided. (16:125)

☐ By Time! Man is indeed in loss, except those who have faith and do righteous deeds, and enjoin one another to follow the truth, and enjoin one another to patience and fortitude. (103:1-5)

☐ And (O Prophet) admonish, for admonition indeed benefits the faithful. (51:55)

☐ You are the best nation ever brought forth for mankind: you bid what is right and forbid what is wrong, and have faith in God. If the People of the Book had believed, it would have been better for them. Among them some are faithful, but most of them are transgressors. (3:110)

☐ God draws another parable: Two men, one of whom is dumb, having no power over anything and who is a liability to his master: wherever he directs him he does not bring any good. Is he equal to someone who enjoins justice and is steady on a straight path? (16:76)

☐ The faithful, men and women, are friends of one another: they bid what is right and forbid what is wrong and maintain the prayer, give the *zakāt*, and obey God and His Apostle. It is they to whom God will soon grant His mercy. God is indeed all-mighty, all-wise. (9:71)

Trust in God

A life lived without trust in God is apt to be full of anxieties in the face of real or imagined dangers and threats, and liable to despair and defeat when faced with challenges. That is because someone who lacks trust imagines that he/she is left to face what he cannot handle by depending on his/her own devices.

When faced with adversities and making decisions and

carrying out important tasks, one must rely on God and ask Him for success. If one does something in this spirit, one's will and prospects will be certainly strong and one will be more confident and optimistic in one's decisions and moves. He/she will finds himself relying on eternal divine power and will not be deterred by obstacles. Trust is the faithful human being's greatest bastion when faced with great challenges.

☐ Those who, when an affliction visits them, say, 'Indeed, we belong to God, and to Him do we indeed return'—it is they who receive the blessings of their Lord and His mercy, and it is they who are the rightly guided. (2:156-157)

☐ Whoever puts his trust in God, He will suffice him. Indeed, God carries through His commands. Certainly God has ordained a measure and extent for everything. (65:3)

☐ Indeed, God loves those who trust in Him. If God helps you, no one can overcome you, but if He forsakes you, who will help you after Him? So in God alone let all the faithful put their trust. (3:159-160)

☐ Whatever you have been given are the wares of the life of this world, but what is with God is better and more lasting for those who have faith and who put their trust in their Lord. (42:36)

☐ The faithful are only those whose hearts tremble with awe when God is mentioned, and when His signs are recited to them, they increase their faith, and who put their trust in their Lord, maintain the prayer and spend out of what We have provided them. It is they who are truly faithful. They shall have ranks near their Lord, forgiveness and a noble provision. (8:2-4)

☐ Put your trust in the Living One, who does not die, and celebrate His praise. He suffices as one all-aware of the sins of

His servants. (25:58)

Remembrance and Supplication

Remembering God and asking for His help will bring joy and peace to the soul. Prayer and remembrance draw human beings closer to God and strengthen their connection with the Source of being, which is the most powerful means of protecting oneself from going astray and becoming infected with sin, corruption and unrighteous conduct. By remembrance of God, our hearts attain calm and our worries and anxieties are allayed.

When a person prays and asks God for help, he or she should observe certain points of etiquette, some of which are mentioned in these verses.

☐ O you who have faith! Remember God with frequent remembrance and glorify Him morning and evening. It is He who blesses you—and so do His angels—that He may bring you out from darkness into light, and He is most merciful to the faithful. (33:41-42)

☐ —Those who have faith and whose hearts find rest in the remembrance of God.' Behold! The hearts find rest solely in God's remembrance! (13:28)

☐ He is the Living One, there is no god except Him. So supplicate Him, putting exclusive faith in Him. All praise belongs to God, Lord of all the nations. (40:65)

☐ When My servants ask you about Me, tell them that I am indeed nearmost. I answer the supplicant's call when he calls Me. So let them respond to Me and have faith in Me, so that they may fare rightly. (2:186)

☐ Your Lord has said, 'Call Me and I will hear you!' Indeed, those who are disdainful of My worship will enter hell in utter humiliation. (40:60)

☐ To God belong the Best Names, so supplicate Him by them, and abandon those who commit sacrilege in His names. Soon they shall be requited for what they used to do. (7:180)

☐ Supplicate your Lord, beseechingly and secretly. Indeed, He does not like the transgressors. Do not cause corruption on the earth after its restoration, and supplicate Him with fear and hope: indeed God's mercy is close to the virtuous. (7:55-56)

☐ Their sides vacate their beds to supplicate their Lord in fear and hope, and they spend out of what We have provided them. (32:16)

☐ And remember Zechariah, when he cried out to his Lord, 'My Lord! Do not leave me without an heir and You are the best of inheritors.' So We answered his prayer and gave him John, and cured for him his wife of infertility. They were indeed active in performing good works, and they would supplicate Us with eagerness and awe and were humble before Us. (21:89-90)

Thanksgiving

One of the biggest harms of polytheism and idolatry, as well as atheism and agnosticism, is that such mind-sets make people oblivious of their real Provider and Sustainer, who is neither acknowledged nor thanked. Ingratitude brings human beings even lower than animals, who might at least know their Provider by instinct. Thanksgiving is the hallmark of authentic and civilized humanity.

Gratitude and appreciation for the opportunities and blessings God has provided to mankind causes individuals to grow in humanity and mature as civilised persons. Anyone who is grateful is thankful for his or her own benefit and will discover the fruits of his or her gratitude. God, too, has promised that if we are grateful for His blessings, He will enhance them, and if we are ungrateful His retribution will be severe.

☐ Remember Me and I will remember you, and thank Me, and do not be ungrateful to Me. (2:152)

☐ (Abraham said to his people who worshipped idols:) What you worship instead of God are mere idols, and you invent a lie. Indeed, those whom you worship besides God have no control over your provision. So seek all your provision from God and worship Him and thank Him, and to Him you shall be brought back.' (29:17)

☐ Eat out of what God has provided you as lawful and good, and give thanks for God's blessing, if it is Him that you worship. (16:114)

☐ … Noah—he was indeed a grateful servant. (17:3)

☐ Indeed, Abraham was a nation [all by himself] obedient to God, a *hanif*, and he was not a polytheist. Grateful [as he was] for His blessings, He chose him and guided him to a straight path. We gave him good in this world, and in the Hereafter he will indeed be among the Righteous. (16:120-122)

☐ Certainly We gave Luqman wisdom, saying, 'Give thanks to God; and whoever gives thanks, gives thanks only for his own sake. And whoever is ungrateful, let him know that God is indeed all-sufficient, all-laudable.' (31:12)

☐ If you are ungrateful, God has indeed no need of you, though He does not approve ingratitude for His servants; and if you give thanks, He approves that for you. No bearer shall bear another's burden; then your return will be to your Lord, whereat He will inform you concerning what you used to do. Indeed, He knows best what is in the breasts. (39:7)

☐ And remember when your Lord declared (to the Israelites), "If you are grateful, I will surely enhance you in blessing, but if you are ungrateful, My punishment is indeed severe." ' (14:7)

Self-Cultivation and Godwariness

Godwariness is the lifeblood of faith. If a person cultivates his soul and purges it from every trace of defilement and darkness, and becomes Godwary by keeping God in his view in all his moves and pauses, decision-making and dealings, such a person will undoubtedly come to possess a great insight and achieve success by being able to avoid every pitfall.

By the side of faith, knowledge and obedience to God and the Apostle, Godwariness and self-cultivation play a basic role in enhancing one's insight about life and destiny, which extend far beyond the transitory and the terrestrial.

▢ God certainly favoured the faithful when He raised up among them an apostle from among themselves to recite to them His signs, and to purify them and teach them the Book and wisdom, and earlier they had indeed been in manifest error. (3:164)

▢ Be wary of God as much as you can, and listen and obey, and spend in the way of God; that is better for yourselves. Those who are saved from their own greed—it is they who are the felicitous. (64:16)

▢ O you who have faith! Be wary of God and let every soul consider what it sends ahead for Tomorrow, and be wary of God. God is indeed well aware of what you do. Do not be like those who forget God, so He makes them forget their own souls. It is they who are the transgressors. (59:18-19)

▢ O you who have faith! Be wary of God with the wariness

due to Him and do not die except in the state of submission [to God and His Apostle]. Hold fast, all together, to God's cord, and do not be divided into sects. Remember God's blessing upon you when you were enemies, then He brought your hearts together, so you became brothers with His blessing. And you were on the brink of a pit of Fire, whereat He saved you from it. Thus does God clarify His signs for you so that you may be guided. (3:102-103)

☐ If the people of the towns had been faithful and Godwary, We would have opened to them blessings from the heaven and the earth. But they impugned Our apostles; so We seized them because of what they used to perpetrate. (7:96)

☐ Whoever is wary of God, He shall make for him a way out [of the adversities of the world and the Hereafter] and provide for him from whence he does not count upon. Whoever puts his trust in God, He will suffice him. Indeed, God carries through His commands. Certainly God has ordained a measure and extent for everything. (65:2-3)

☐ And this Book We have sent down is a blessed one; so follow it and be Godwary so that you may receive His mercy. (6:155)

☐ 'O Children of Adam! We have certainly sent down to you garments to cover your nakedness, and for adornment. Yet the garment of Godwariness—that is the best.' That is one of God's signs, so that they may take admonition. (7:26)

☐ O you who have faith! If you are wary of God, He will appoint a criterion for you, and absolve you of your misdeeds and forgive you, for God is dispenser of a mighty grace. (8:29)

☐ O you who have faith! Be wary of God, and be with the Truthful. (9:119)

☐ 'Felicitous is he who purifies himself, celebrates the

Name of his Lord, and prays. Rather, you prefer the life of this world, while the Hereafter is better and more lasting.' This is indeed in the former scriptures, the scriptures of Abraham and Moses. (87:14-19)

☐ O you who have faith! Be maintainers of justice, as witnesses for God's sake,d and ill feeling for a people should never lead you to be unfair. Be fair; that is nearer to Godwariness, and be wary of God. God is indeed well aware of what you do. (5:8)

☐ Whoever obeys God and His Apostle and fears God and is wary of Him—it is they who will be triumphant. (24:52)

☐ By the soul and Him who fashioned it, and inspired it with discernment between its virtues and vices: one who purifies it is felicitous and one who betrays it fails. (91:7-10)

Patience and Perseverance

One of the ways of success, both in religious and secular matters, is patience, endurance and perseverance. With patience and perseverance, one can achieve many goals in life and reach the highest spiritual levels through divine assistance.

☐ O you who have faith! Be patient, stand firm, and close your ranks, and be wary of God so that you may be felicitous. (3:200)

☐ (O Prophet,) be steadfast, just as you have been commanded—you and whoever has turned to God with you—and do not overstep the bounds. Indeed, He watches what you do. Do not incline toward the wrongdoers, lest the Fire should touch you, and you will not have any protector besides God; then you will not be helped. (11:112-113)

☐ (O Muslims,) obey God and His Apostle and do not

dispute, or you will lose heart and your power will be gone. And be patient; indeed God is with the patient. (8:46)

☐ When they (i.e., the Israelites) had been patient and had conviction in Our signs, We appointed amongst them leaders to guide the people by Our command. (32:24)

☐ Indeed, those who say, 'Our Lord is God!' and then remain steadfast, the angels descend upon them, saying, 'Do not fear, nor be grieved! Receive the good news of the paradise which you have been promised. (41:30)

☐ As for those who strive in Us, We shall surely guide them in Our ways, and God is indeed with the virtuous. (29:69)

☐ Those who are patient for the sake of their Lord's pleasure, maintain the prayer, and spend secretly and openly out of what We have provided them, and repel others' evil conduct with good. For such will be the reward of the ultimate abode: (13:22)

Loving God's Friends, the Role Models

One of the factors of spiritual growth and ascent toward God is identifying oneself with God's Friends and holy personages and following them as role models. This can happen when we love them. In these verses, people are asked to associate and keep company with those who call on God, and the Prophet in particular is introduced as a good exemplar for the faithful.

☐ Content yourself with the company of those who supplicate their Lord morning and evening, desiring His Face, and do not loose sight of them, desiring the glitter of the life of this world. And do not obey him whose heart We have made oblivious to Our remembrance and who follows his base desires, and whose conduct is mere profligacy. (18:28)

☐ They (i.e., the prophets of old, from Noah to Jesus) are the ones whom We gave the Book, judgement and prophethood. So if these (Arabs) disbelieve in them, We have certainly entrusted them to a people who will never disbelieve in them. They are the ones whom God has guided. So follow their guidance.

Say (O Prophet), 'I do not ask you any recompense for it. It is just an admonition for all the nations.' (6:89-90)

☐ There is certainly a good exemplar for you in the Apostle of God—for those who look forward to God and the Last Day and remember God much. (33:21)

☐ There is certainly a good exemplar for you in Abraham and those who were with him, when they said to their own people, 'We indeed repudiate you and whatever you worship besides God. We disown you, and enmity and hate have appeared between you and us for ever, unless you come to have faith in God alone,' apart from Abraham's saying to his father, 'I will surely plead forgiveness for you, though I cannot avail you anything against God.'

They prayed, 'Our Lord! In You do we put our trust, to You do we turn penitently, and toward You is the destination. Our Lord! Do not make us a test for the faithless, and forgive us. Our Lord! Indeed, You are the All-mighty, the All-wise.'

There is certainly a good exemplar for you in them—for those who look forward to God and the Last Day—and anyone who refuses to comply should know that God is indeed the All-sufficient, the All-laudable. (60:4-6)

☐ Say (O Prophet), 'If you love God, then follow me; God will love you and forgive you your sins, and God is all-forgiving, all-merciful.' (3:31)

☐ O you who have faith! Be wary of God, and be with the Truthful. (9:119)

☐ The faithful, men and women, are friends of one another: they bid what is right and forbid what is wrong and maintain the prayer, give the *zakāt*, and obey God and His Apostle. It is they to whom God will soon grant His mercy. God is indeed all-mighty, all-wise. (9:71)

☐ The early vanguard of the Emigrants and the Helpers and those who followed them in virtue—God is pleased with them and they are pleased with Him, and He has prepared for them gardens with streams running in them, to remain in them forever. That is the great success. (9:100)

Forgiving Others' Trespasses and Faults

Forgiveness is one of the moral virtues recommended by the Qur'an. One must exercise self-control and patience in relation to the faults of others and excuse them, just as one expects God to forgive one's faults. Forgiveness means suppressing one's anger and confronting others' misconduct with patience and forbearance. The Qur'an has invited everyone to this virtuous trait.

☐ It is by God's mercy that you (O Prophet) are gentle to them; had you been harsh and hard-hearted, they would have surely scattered from around you. So excuse them and plead for forgiveness for them, and consult them in the affairs, and once you are resolved, put your trust in God. Indeed, God loves those who trust in Him. (3:159)

☐ Adopt a policy of excusing the faults of people, bid what is right, and turn away from the ignorant. (7:199)

☐ The well-off and opulent among you should not vow that they will give no more to the relatives, the needy, and those who have migrated in the way of God; let them excuse and forbear. Do you not love that God should forgive you? God is all-forgiving, all-merciful. (24:22)

☐ —Those who spend in ease and adversity, and suppress their anger, and excuse the faults of the people, and God loves the virtuous; and those who, when they commit an indecent act or wrong themselves, remember God, and plead to God seeking forgiveness for their sins—and who forgives sins except God? (3:134)

Gentleness in Behaviour and Polite Speech

Ill temper and abusive behaviour is one of the worst ethical vices and has harmful effects on human relationships, disrupting inner peace and making life bitter. On the contrary, gentleness, tolerance, kindness and geniality are factors of a cheerful environment and social acceptance. The Qur'an invites both the Prophet and the Muslims to gentleness and self-restraint, and regards gentleness in behaviour and speech as an important factor of felicity.

☐ Tell My servants to speak in a manner which is the best. Indeed, Satan incites ill feeling between them, and Satan is indeed man's open enemy. (17:53)

☐ The servants of the All-beneficent are those who walk humbly on the earth, and when the ignorant address them, say, 'Peace!' (25:63)

☐ Both of you (i.e., Moses and Aaron) go to Pharaoh, for he has indeed rebelled. Speak to him in a soft manner; maybe he will take admonition or fear.' (20:43-44)

☐ It is by God's mercy that you (O Prophet) are gentle to them; had you been harsh and hard-hearted, they would have surely scattered from around you. So excuse them and plead for forgiveness for them, and consult them in the affairs, and once you are resolved, put your trust in God. Indeed, God loves those who trust in Him. (3:159)

☐ When you are greeted with a salute, greet with a better one than it, or return it; indeed God takes account of all things. (4:86)

☐ Do not turn your cheek away disdainfully from the people, and do not walk boastfully on the earth. Indeed, God does not like any swaggering braggart. Be modest in your bearing, and lower your voice. Indeed, the ungainliest of voices is the donkey's voice.' (31:18-19)

☐ O you who have faith! Should any of you desert his religion, God will soon bring a people whom He loves and who love Him, who will be humble towards the faithful, stern towards the faithless, struggling in the way of God, not fearing the blame of any blamer. That is God's grace which He grants to whomever He wishes, and God is all-bounteous, all-knowing. (5:54)

☐ A polite reply to the needy and forgiving their annoyance is better than a charity followed by affront. God is all-sufficient, most forbearing. (2:263)

Sympathetic Advice and Good Faith

Advice and guidance to others through sympathy and benevolence is one of the ethical virtues of God's prophets. Speaking out of good faith and goodwill disarms even the enemy and removes hatred from the hearts. In the Holy Qur'an, benevolence and exhortation are introduced as the attributes of the prophets and everyone should take an example from them. Advice and benevolence must first start from the family and those around one, and then reach out to others.

☐ When Luqman said to his son, as he advised him: 'O

my son! Do not ascribe any partners to God. Polytheism is indeed a great injustice.' (31:13)

☐ (Noah said to his people), I communicate the messages of my Lord to you and I am your well-wisher, and I know from God what you do not know. (7:62)

☐ Who has a better call than him who summons to God and acts righteously and says, 'I am indeed one of those have submitted to God'?
Good and evil conduct are not equal. Repel evil with what is best. If you do so, he between whom and you was enmity, will be as though he were a sympathetic friend. But none is granted it except those who are patient, and none is granted it except the greatly endowed. (41:33-35)

☐ So he (i.e., the Prophet Salih) abandoned them to their fate, and said, 'O my people! Certainly I communicated to you the message of my Lord, and I was your well-wisher, but you did not like well-wishers.' (7:79)

☐ O mankind! There has certainly come to you an advice from your Lord, and cure for what is in the breasts, and guidance and mercy for the faithful. (10:57)

☐ (O Prophet,) admonish, for admonition indeed benefits the faithful. (51:55)

Cooperation and Teamwork

According to Islam, the members of the community must cooperate with one another in sponsoring worthy goals and refrain from supporting detrimental objectives. With the help and participation of one another they should move forward and serve one another and overcome problems by pooling their resources.

The verses chosen here emphasize this, and the faithful, as brethren, are also obliged to make peace between themselves and to urged to surpass each other in doing good deeds.

☐ O you who have faith! … Cooperate in piety and God-wariness, but do not cooperate in sin and aggression, and be wary of God. God is indeed severe in retribution. (5:2)

☐ O you who have faith! Be patient, stand firm, and close your ranks, and be wary of God so that you may be felicitous. (3:200)

☐ Is it they who dispense the mercy of your Lord? It is We who have dispensed among them their livelihood in the present life and raised some of them above others in rank, so that some may take others into service, and your Lord's mercy is better than what they amass. (43:32)

☐ The faithful are indeed brothers. Therefore, make peace between your brothers and be wary of God, so that you may receive His mercy. (49:10)

Respect for Others' Privacy

From the point of view of the Qur'an, everyone's personal privacy should be protected and no one should compromise his or her private life. One should not enter a house without permission and return if told not to enter without considering it as a discourtesy. Even children should get permission when they enter their parent's room.

Also, it is also not permissible to spy on someone's life, and to reveal the secrets of others.

☐ O you who have faith! Do not enter houses other than your own until you have announced your arrival and greeted their occupants. That is better for you. Maybe you will take admonition. But if you do not find anyone in them, do not enter them until you are given permission. And if you are told: 'Turn back,' then do turn back. That will be more decent on your part. God knows best what you do. (24:27-28)

▢   O you who have faith! Your slaves and those of you who have not yet reached puberty should seek your permission at three times: before the dawn prayer, and when you put off your garments at noon, and after the night prayer. These are three times of privacy for you. Apart from these, it is not sinful of you or them to frequent one another freely. Thus does God clarify the signs for you, and God is all-knowing, all-wise. (24:58)

▢   And do not obey any vile swearer, scandal-monger, talebearer, hinderer of all good, sinful transgressor, callous and, on top of that, base-born —who behaves thus only because he has wealth and children. When Our signs are recited to him, he says, 'Myths of the ancients!' Soon We shall brand him on his snout. (68:10-16)

▢   It is not piety that you enter the houses from their rear; rather, piety is personified by one who is Godwary, and enter the houses from their doors, and be wary of God, so that you may be felicitous. (2:189)

Strengthening the Family System

Human society is made up of families, and Islam believes in a special sanctity and status for the family, giving special importance to the Islamic life style within it and setting forth various ordinances to strengthen the family's foundations.

These verses speak of love and compassion as the foundations of the family, the necessity of marrying off the youth, the mutual duties of husband and wife, and the manner of resolving their differences and disagreements. They point out the necessity of properly educating the children, saving them from falling into erroneous ways, and the responsibility of the head of the family towards other members.

☐ And of His signs is that He created for you mates from your own selves that you may take comfort in them, and He ordained affection and mercy between you. There are indeed signs in that for a people who reflect. (30:21)

☐ It is He who created the human being from water, then invested him with ties of blood and marriage, and your Lord is all-powerful. (25:54)

☐ God made for you mates from your own selves and appointed for you children and grandchildren from your mates, and We provided you with all the good things. What, do they believe in falsehood while they deny the blessing of God? (16:72)

☐ Marry off those who are single among you, and the upright among your male and female slaves. If they are poor, God will enrich them out of His bounty, and God is all-bounteous, all-knowing. (24:32)

☐ Men are the managers of women, because of the advantage God has granted some of them over others, and by virtue of their spending out of their wealth. Righteous women are obedient and watchful in the absence of their husbands of what God has enjoined them to guard. As for those wives whose misconduct you fear, first advise them, and [if ineffective] keep away from them in the bed, and [as the last resort] beat them.[1] Then if they obey you, do not seek any course of action against them. Indeed, God is all-exalted, all-great. (4:34)

☐ If a woman fears misconduct or desertion from her husband, there is no sin upon the couple if they reach a reconciliation between themselves; and reconciliation is better. The

---

[1] Or 'snub them,' 'give them the cold shoulder.'

souls are prone to greed; but if you are virtuous and Godwary, God is indeed well aware of what you do. (4:128)

☐ And those who say, 'Our Lord! Give us joy and comfort in our spouses and offspring, and make us leaders of the Godwary.' (25:74)

☐ O mankind! Be wary of your Lord, who created you from a single soul, and created its mate from it, and, from the two of them, scattered numerous men and women. Be wary of God, in whose Name you adjure one another and of severing the ties with blood relations. God is indeed watchful over you. (4:1)

☐ Mothers shall suckle their children for two full years—that for such as desire to complete the suckling—and on the father shall be their maintenance and clothing, in accordance with honourable norms. No soul is to be tasked except according to its capacity: neither the mother shall be made to suffer harm on her child's account, nor the father on account of his child, and on the father's heir devolve duties and rights similar to that. And if the couple desire to wean, with mutual consent and consultation, there will be no sin upon them. And if you want to have your children wet-nursed, there will be no sin upon you so long as you pay what you give in accordance with honourable norms, and be wary of God and know that God watches what you do. (2:233)

☐ O you who have faith! Save yourselves and your families from a Fire whose fuel will be people and stones, over which are assigned severe and mighty angels, who do not disobey whatever God commands them and carry out what they are commanded. (66:6)

☐ (O Prophet) bid your family to prayer and be steadfast in maintaining it. We do not ask any provision of you: it is We who provide for you, and the ultimate outcome in the Hereafter belongs to Godwariness. (20:132)

☐ We have enjoined man to be kind to his parents. His mother has carried him in travail and bore him in travail, and his gestation and weaning take thirty months. When he comes of age and reaches forty years, he says, 'My Lord! Inspire me to give thanks for Your blessing with which You have blessed me and my parents, and that I may do righteous deeds which please You, and invest my descendants with righteousness. I have indeed turned to you in penitence, and I am one of those who have submitted to You.' (46:15)

The Etiquette of Speaking and Listening; Disinformation

Speaking and listening are two important means of communicating with others and understanding them, and from the viewpoint of the Qur'an there are certain points of etiquette that must be observed. One should speak clearly and gracefully and on the basis of facts, so that his or her words can have a favourable effect on the listener.

While listening to the Word of God it is necessary to maintain silence, to listen well and with the intent to obey it. Also, while listening to the opinions of the people, one must listen to them all, but choose the best among them. If an unreliable person makes statements or brings some news, which may be fake news, one must not jump to a conclusion immediately, but investigate the matter before making any judgement.

☐ O you who have faith! Be wary of God and speak upright words. He will rectify your conduct for you and forgive you your sins. Whoever obeys God and His Apostle will certainly achieve a great success. (33:70-71)

☐ They have been guided to chaste speech, and guided to the path of the All-laudable. (22:24)

☐ When the Qur'ān is recited, listen to it and be silent, maybe you will receive God's mercy. (7:204)

☐ Tell My servants to speak in a manner which is the best. Indeed, Satan incites ill feeling between them, and Satan is indeed man's open enemy. (17:53)

☐ Remember God's blessing upon you and His covenant with which He has bound you when you said, 'We hear and obey.' And be wary of God. Indeed, God knows well what is in the breasts. (5:7)

☐ All the response of the faithful, when they are summoned to God and His Apostle that He may judge between them, is to say, 'We hear and obey.' It is they who will be felicitous. Whoever obeys God and His Apostle and fears God and is wary of Him—it is they who will be triumphant. (24:51-52)

☐ So give good news to My servants who listen to the word of God and follow the best interpretation of it. They are the ones whom God has guided and it is they who possess intellect. (39:17-18)

☐ 'Our Lord, we have indeed heard a summoner calling to faith, declaring, "Have faith in your Lord!" So we believed. Our Lord, forgive us our sins and absolve us of our misdeeds, and make us die with the pious.' (3:193)

☐ O you who have faith! If a vicious character brings you some news, verify it, lest you should visit harm on some people out of ignorance, and then become regretful for what you have done. (49:06)

Humility and Good Morals

A Muslim must be humble and genial towards others. Having good morals is one of the important teachings of Islam. A friendly disposition averts hostility and resentment and gives way to friendship. One of the reasons for the influence and popularity of God's Prophet among the people was his good morals and gentle manners.

Muslims must always follow the example of that Prophet.

☐ Do not walk exultantly on the earth. Indeed, you will neither pierce the earth, nor reach the mountains in height. The evil of all these is detestable to your Lord. (17:37-38)

☐ Muhammad, the Apostle of God, and those who are with him are hard against the faithless and merciful amongst themselves. You see them bowing and prostrating in worship, seeking God's grace and His pleasure. Their mark is visible on their faces, from the effect of prostration. Such is their description in the Torah and their description in the Gospel: like a tillage that sends out its shoots and builds them up, and they grow stout and settle on their stalks, impressing the sowers, so that He may enrage the faithless by them. God has promised those of them who have faith and do righteous deeds forgiveness and a great reward. (48:29)

☐ It is by God's mercy that you (O Prophet) are gentle to them; had you been harsh and hard-hearted, they would have surely scattered from around you. So excuse them and plead for forgiveness for them, and consult them in the affairs, and once you are resolved, put your trust in God. Indeed, God loves those who trust in Him. (3:159)

☐ There is certainly a good exemplar for you in the Apostle of God—for those who look forward to God and the Last Day and remember God much. (33:21)

☐ Tell My servants to speak in a manner which is the best. Indeed, Satan incites ill feeling between them, and Satan is indeed man's open enemy. (17:53)

☐ (O Prophet,) do not extend your glance toward what We have provided to certain groups of them, and do not grieve for them. Lower your wing to the faithful, (15:88)

☐ Those (i.e., the righteous among Jews and Christians who accept the Qur'an as God's Word) will be given their reward two times for their patience. They repel evil conduct with good, and spend out of what We have provided them, (28:54)

☐ O you who have faith! When you are told, 'Make room,' in sittings, then do make room; God will make room for you. And when you are told, 'Rise up!' Do rise up. God will raise in rank those of you who have faith and those who have been given knowledge, and God is well aware of what you do. (58:11)

Greeting Others

Greeting others is an important means of creating affection and familiarity among individuals in the community. When one is greeted by another, in fact, he wishes for his welfare and well-being. In the Qur'an, the Prophet of God is commanded to greet the faithful when they come to him, and the faithful, too, are commanded, when they enter a house, to say greetings to its inmates, and to respond in a better manner when greeted by someone.

☐ When you are greeted with a salute, greet with a better one than it, or return it; indeed God takes account of all things. (4:86)

☐ O you who have faith! Do not enter houses other than your own until you have announced your arrival and greeted their occupants. That is better for you. Maybe you will take admonition. (24:27)

☐ There will be no blame on you whether you eat together or separately. So when you enter houses, greet yourselves with a salutation from God, blessed and good. Thus does God clarify His signs for you so that you may exercise your reason. (24:61)

☐   Seek the abode of the Hereafter by the means that God has given you, while not forgetting your share of this world. Be good to others just as God has been good to you, and do not try to cause corruption in the land. Indeed, God does not like the agents of corruption.' (28:77)

☐   When the division (of a deceased person's legacy) is attended by relatives, the orphans and the needy, provide for them out of it, and speak to them honourable words. (4:8)

☐   Did you receive the story of Abraham's honoured guests? When they entered into his presence, they said, 'Peace!' 'Peace!' He answered, 'You are an unfamiliar folk.' (51:24-25)

☐   O you who have faith! When you issue forth in the way of God, try to ascertain: do not say to someone who offers you peace, 'You are not a believer,' seeking the transitory wares of the life of this world. But with God are plenteous gains. You too were such earlier, but God did you a favour. Therefore, do ascertain. God is indeed well aware of what you do. (4:94)

☐   The servants of the All-beneficent are those who walk humbly on the earth, and when the ignorant address them, say, 'Peace!' (25:63)

☐   And when they (i.e., proto-Muslims, who belonged to the pre-Islamic Jewish and Christian communities) hear vain talk they avoid it and say, 'Our deeds belong to us and your deeds belong to you. Peace be to you. We do not court the ignorant.' (28:55)

Cleanliness and Tidy Appearance

Just as one's inner self must be pure and luminous, one's appearance must be neat. Cleanliness and tidiness of clothing and body are recommended in Islam. Muslims must wash their hands and faces several times daily for prayers, and, at times, it is obligatory to wash the whole body, and desirable at some other times.[1]

It is appropriate for a Muslim to dress up when attending any mosque and no one has the right to forbid the ornament that God has created for His servants.

☐ O you wrapped up in your mantle! Rise up and warn! Magnify your Lord, purify your clothes. (74:1-4)

☐ O you who have faith! When you stand up for prayer, wash your faces and your hands up to the elbows, and wipe a part of your heads and your feet up to the ankles. If you are *junub*,[2] purify yourselves. (5:6)

☐ O Children of Adam! Put on your adornment on every occasion of prayer, and eat and drink, but do not waste; indeed He does not like the wasteful. Say, 'Who has forbidden the adornment of God, which He has brought forth for His servants, and the good things of His provision?' Say, 'These are for the faithful in the life of this world, and exclusively for them on the Day of Resurrection.' Thus do We elaborate the signs for a people who have knowledge. (7:31-32)

☐ A mosque founded on Godwariness from the very first day is worthier that you stand in it for prayer. Therein are men who love to keep pure, and God loves those who keep pure. (9:108)

---

[1] Such as on Fridays, festivals and holy occasions and when visiting shrines.
[2] That is, in the state of *janābah*, or major ritual impurity arising from sexual intercourse, or touching a corpse.

Part Three
The Laws of the Qur'an

CHAPTER 10

Obligations and Ordinances

Law, in its holistic sense, had an important function in Torah and the Mosaic faith, covering various aspects of individual and social behaviour, relationships, interaction and activities, including belief, study of Torah, rites of purification, offerings, taxes, Temple affairs, laws governing work, holidays, diet, clothing, business dealings, contracts, matters dealing with penal law, war and peace.[1] It was the significance of law as central to Jewish life and its continued study by rabbinical Judaism that played a crucial role in the survival of the Jewish religion, scholarship and identity through the centuries after the destruction of the Second Temple and dispersion of the Palestinian community under Roman rule.

However, law plays no such significant role in the New Testament and the Christian religion. In fact, the primary force of the teaching of Paul, as he was understood to be setting forth in his letters, which shaped mainstream Christianity as a breakaway creed, was directed to nullify the role of Mosaic Law, to spare the Gentile proselytes the 'burden' of following Jewish rites and customs, such

---

1 The variety of the concerns of Mosaic law is reflected in the lists of 613 *mitzvot*, or commandments, compiled by the Rabbis. See the related Wikipedia article at: https://en.wikipedia.org/wiki/613_commandments.

as circumcision and food laws.[1]

The Qur'an revives in its teachings the weakened role of religious law under Christianity. Hundreds of its verses serve as a rich mine for deduction of religious rules and legal principles that extend to almost all spheres of life, public and private. The Holy Qur'an is a major source of religious law for Muslim communities, and Muslim sects have developed at least six major schools of jurisprudence.

Obedience to God and the Apostle

One of the factors responsible for the all-round growth of human beings is complete and continuous obedience to God and His Prophet. This obligation to obey God's commands and those of His Apostle is a basic principle underlying the practice of Islamic law and ethics. God has promised in many verses, including the following, that

---

[1] However, as no durable system, religious or secular, can do without some kind of legal code, the Roman Catholic Church developed the canon law as a system of laws and legal principles made and enforced by the ecclesiastical authorities to regulate church organization and governance and to order the activities of Catholics in sacramental, liturgical, matrimonial, penal and other matter dealing with church discipline. It subscribes not just to the norms of the New Testament, but includes elements of the Hebrew, Roman, Visigothic and other legal traditions. toward the mission of the Church. The 1983 Code of Canon Law, promulgated on 25 January 1983 by John Paul II, is the second and current codification of canonical legislation for the Latin Church.

The other 23 *sui iuris* Churches, which collectively make up the Eastern Catholic Churches, follow the Code of Canons of the Eastern Churches (CCEO), promulgated on 18 October 1990 by Pope John Paul II. It is a document in Latin, divided into 30 titles and has a total of 1546 canons.

Protestant denominations and churches have their own codes meant to regulate organisation, procedures, worship and practice at different levels.

those who obey Him and follow His Prophet and strive for His cause will partake of His mercy and be guided in His paths. It is in this state that human beings attain a better and sharpened understanding with divine approval.

☐ Obey God and the Apostle so that you may be granted His mercy. Hasten towards your Lord's forgiveness and a paradise as vast as the heavens and the earth, prepared for the Godwary. (3:132-133)

☐ Say, 'Obey God and obey the Apostle.' But if you turn your backs, you should know that he (i.e., the Prophet) is only responsible for his burden and you are responsible for your own burden, and if you obey him, you will be guided, and the Apostle's duty is only to communicate in clear terms. (24:54)

☐ As for those who strive in Us, We shall surely guide them in Our ways, and God is indeed with the virtuous. (29:69)

☐ The faithful, men and women, are friends of one another: they bid what is right and forbid what is wrong and maintain the prayer, give the *zakāt*, and obey God and His Apostle. It is they to whom God will soon grant His mercy. God is indeed all-mighty, all-wise. (9:71)

☐ Whoever obeys God and the Apostle—they are with those whom God has blessed, including the prophets and the truthful, the martyrs and the righteous, and excellent companions are they! That is the grace of God, and God suffices as knower of His creatures. (4:69-70)

☐ Whoever obeys God and His Apostle and fears God and is wary of Him—it is they who will be triumphant. (24:52)

Learning the Laws

The health and vigour of a religious community depends on the extent to which the common people know and practice the laws. The Torah enjoins upon its followers to learn the God-given commandments in these words:

> ☐ These commandments that I give you today are to be upon your hearts. Impress them on your children. Talk about them when you sit at home and when you walk along the road, when you lie down and when you get up. Tie them as symbols on your hands and bind them on your foreheads. Write them on the door frames of your houses and on your gates. (Deuteronomy 6:6-9)

The Qur'an repeatedly refers to how the Israelites were urged to hold fast to the Scripture, as the following two examples show.

> ☐ We wrote for Moses in the Tablets advice concerning all things and an elaboration of all things, and We said, 'Hold on to them with power, and bid your people to hold on to the best of what is in them.' (7:145)

> ☐ When We took a pledge from you (Israelites), and raised the Mount above you declaring, 'Hold on with power to what We have given you and remember that which is in it so that you may be Godwary.'

One of the main duties of Muslims is to learn the laws of Islam. A brief knowledge is essential for everyone, and detailed study is the collective duty of the community, to be to met by groups of individuals devoted to pursuing scholarship. This means a group of students must go forth from every community to seek scholarly knowledge of religion and return to teach and guide their own people. One of the important duties of the prophets was to instruct the people in scriptures and wisdom.

> ☐ We did not send any apostles before you (O Muham-

mad) except as men to whom We revealed. (O people,) ask the People of the Reminder[1] if you do not know. We sent them with clear proofs and scriptures. We have sent down the Reminder to you (O Muhammad) so that you may clarify for these people that which has been sent down to them, so that they may reflect. (16:43-44)

☐ It is He who sent to the unlettered people an apostle from among themselves, to recite to them His signs, to purify them, and to teach them the Book and wisdom, and earlier they had indeed been in manifest error. (62:02)

☐ Yet it is not for the faithful to go forth *en masse*. But why should not a group from each of their sections go forth to become learned in religion and to warn their people when they return to them, so that they may beware? (9:122)

Justice and Fairness

One of the important teachings of Islam is to observe justice and fairness in all affairs. In an Islamic society, the rulers and authorities must be just, and, in addition, all people must act fairly in their daily lives, and this has been one of the high goals of the prophetic missions.

The Holy Qur'an has called for justice even in the treatment of enemies. One of the most important ideals of the Qur'an is justice and fair dealing. Even where there is oppression, the oppressed can retaliate in proportion to the amount of wrong he/she has suffered; he must observe justice and avoid excessive measures. Iron and steel have been put at man's disposal to uphold divine ideals, not to oppress other communities and nations in the pursuit of imperialist objectives.

☐ O you who have faith! Be maintainers of justice, as wit-

---
[1] That is, sages and scholars of former divine creeds.

nesses for God's sake, and ill feeling for a people should never lead you to be unfair. Be fair; that is nearer to Godwariness, and be wary of God. God is indeed well aware of what you do. (5:8)

☐ Certainly We sent Our apostles with clear proofs, and We sent down with them the Book and the Balance, so that mankind may maintain justice; and We sent down iron, in which there is great might and uses for mankind, and so that God may know those who help Him and His apostles with faith in the Unseen. God is indeed all-strong, all-mighty. (57:25)

☐ Indeed, God commands you to deliver the trusts to their rightful owners, and to judge with fairness when you judge between people. Excellent indeed is what God advises you. God is indeed all-hearing, all-seeing. (4:58)

☐ Do not approach the orphan's property, except in the best possible manner, until he comes of age. Observe fully the measure and the balance with justice. We task no soul except according to its capacity.

And when you speak, be just, even if it were a relative; and fulfil God's covenants. This is what He enjoins upon you so that you may take admonition. (6:152)

☐ Indeed, God enjoins justice and kindness, and generosity towards relatives, and He forbids indecency, wrongdoing, and aggression. He advises you so that you may take admonition. (16:90)

☐ God does not forbid you from dealing with kindness and justice with those polytheists who did not make war against you on account of religion and did not expel you from your homes. God indeed loves the just. (60:08)

☐ A sacred month for a sacred month, and all sanctities require retribution. So should anyone aggress against you, assail him in the manner he assailed you, and be wary of God, and know that God is with the Godwary. (2:194)

☐ If two groups of the faithful fight one another, make peace between them. But if one party of them aggresses against the other, fight the one which aggresses until it returns to God's ordinance. Then, if it returns, make peace between them fairly, and do justice. God indeed loves the just. (49:9)

Duty to Urge Rightful & Forbid Wrongful Conduct

Bidding others to do what is good and right, and to forbid what is evil and wrong, this two-fold duty has been prescribed to encourage right conduct and to protect the society from any kind of deviation, pollution and sin. The duty applies to the ruling authorities as well as the common citizens. Every Muslim, if he/she fulfils the necessary requirements, is obliged to invite and urge others to do good and to bid them to fulfil their obligations, and to forbid if he/she sees any evil and deviation in society. This duty, with its special conditions, can guarantee the betterment of society and its spiritual health and can be very effective in creating a wholesome living environment.

☐ There has to be a nation among you summoning to the good, bidding what is right, and forbidding what is wrong. It is they who are the felicitous. (3:104)

☐ You are the best nation[1] ever brought forth for mankind: you bid what is right and forbid what is wrong, and have faith in God. And if the People of the Book had believed, it would have been better for them. Among them some are faithful, but most of them are transgressors. (3:110)

☐ Among the People of the Book[2] is an upright nation;

---

[1] Or 'leaders,' according to an alternate reading.
[2] The expression 'People of the Book' here, as is apparent from the context,

they recite God's signs[1] in the watches of the night and prostrate. They have faith in God and the Last Day, and bid what is right and forbid what is wrong, and they are active in performing good deeds. Those are among the righteous. (3:114)

☐ The faithful, men and women, are friends of one another: they bid what is right and forbid what is wrong and maintain the prayer, give the *zakāt*, and obey God and His Apostle. It is they to whom God will soon grant His mercy. God is indeed all-mighty, all-wise. (9:71)

☐ For every nation We have appointed rites of worship which they observe; so let them not dispute with you about your religion. And invite to your Lord. You are indeed on a straight guidance. (22:67)

☐ Those who follow the Apostle, the untaught prophet, whose mention they find written with them in the Torah and the Gospel, who bids them to do what is right and forbids them from what is wrong, makes lawful to them all the good things and forbids them from all vicious things, and relieves them of their burdens and the shackles that were upon them—those who believe in him, honour him, and help him and follow the light that has been sent down with him, they are the felicitous.' (7:157)

☐ Will you bid others to piety and forget yourselves, while you recite the Book? Do you not exercise your reason? (2:44)

☐ Why were there not among the generations before you a remnant of the wise who might forbid corruption in the land, except a few of those whom We delivered from among them? Those who were wrongdoers pursued gratification in the means of affluence they had been granted, and they were a guilty lot. (11:116)

---

refers to the Jewish community.

[1] That is, the Hebrew scripture.

Consultation

Consultation is of vital importance, both on the level of public affairs, as well as in personal matters. Republics and democracies, which function on the basis of the participation of the people and popular consent in governance of public affairs are more successful in achieving political, economic and social goals and harmony than monarchies and despotic regimes.

The Holy Qur'an considers consultation to be one of the ways of life for the faithful and, more significantly, commands even the Prophet of Islam to consult with the people in public affairs. Also in personal matters and relationships, one gains by consulting others from their experiences and wisdom.

☐ (The faithful are) those who answer their Lord, maintain the prayer, and conduct their affairs by counsel among themselves, and they spend out of what We have provided them; those who, when afflicted by aggression, defend themselves. (42:38-39)

☐ It is by God's mercy that you (O Prophet) are gentle to them; had you been harsh and hard-hearted, they would have surely scattered from around you. So excuse them and plead for forgiveness for them, and consult them in the affairs, and once you are resolved, put your trust in God. Indeed, God loves those who trust in Him. (3:159)

Loyalty to Trusts and Agreements

An important feature of Islamic conduct is trustworthiness, and the Qur'an commands it in strong terms. The Muslim, as individuals and community, must return whatever kind of trust they is entrusted with, and remain loyal to every agreement and compact they make.

According to the Qur'an, one who betrays a trust and breaks his covenant is worthy of anathema and punishment.

☐ Indeed, God commands you to deliver the trusts to their rightful owners, and to judge with fairness when you judge between people. Excellent indeed is what God advises you. God is indeed all-hearing, all-seeing. (4:58)

☐ ... And those who keep their trusts and covenants and are watchful of their prayers. It is they who will be the inheritors, who shall inherit paradise and will remain in it. (23:8-11)

☐ Do not approach the orphan's property except in the best manner, until he comes of age. Fulfil your covenants; indeed all covenants are accountable. (17:34)

☐ Fulfil God's covenant when you pledge, and do not break your oaths after pledging them solemnly and having made God a witness over yourselves. God indeed knows what you do. (16:91)

☐ Yes, whoever fulfils his commitments and is wary of God—God indeed loves the Godwary. (3:76)

Sincerity and Intent of Nearness to God

Every kind of worship and good deed by a human being is valuable if it is for the sake of God, otherwise it has no worth in God's sight. The intention to attain nearness to God and acting for the sake of God alone are the basic condition of acceptance of any form of worship. But if it is done to show off, for the sake of name or material gain, it is worthless and futile, and God will not accept or reward it.

In these verses, people are told to do whatever good

work they do for the sake of God and for His good pleasure.

☐ We have indeed sent down the Book to you (O Prophet) with the truth; so worship God, putting exclusive faith in Him. Indeed, only exclusive faith is worthy of God, and those who take others as masters besides Him claiming, 'We only worship them so that they may bring us near to God,' God will judge between them concerning that about which they differ. Indeed, God does not guide someone who is a liar and an ingrate. (39:2-3)

☐ It is He who shows you His signs and sends down provision for you from the sky. Yet no one takes admonition except those who return penitently to God. So supplicate God putting exclusive faith in Him, though the faithless should be averse. (40:13-14)

☐ Say, 'I am just a human being like you. It has been revealed to me that your God is the One God. So whoever expects to encounter his Lord, let him act righteously and not associate anyone with the worship of his Lord.' (18:110)

☐ And they say, 'No one will enter paradise except one who is a Jew or Christian.' Those are their false hopes! Say, 'Produce your evidence, should you be truthful.' Certainly whoever submits his will to God and is virtuous, he shall have his reward with his Lord, and they will have no fear, nor shall they grieve. (2:112)

☐ The parable of those who spend their wealth seeking God's pleasure and to confirm themselves in their faith, is that of a garden on a hillside: the downpour strikes it, whereupon it brings forth its fruit twofold; and if it is not a downpour that strikes it, then a shower, and God watches what you do. (2:265)

☐ … And those who join what God has commanded to be

joined, fear their Lord, and are afraid of an adverse reckoning —those who are patient for the sake of their Lord's pleasure, maintain the prayer, and spend secretly and openly out of what We have provided them, and repel others' evil conduct with good. For such will be the reward of the ultimate abode: (13:21-22)

☐ Say (O Prophet), 'Indeed, my prayer and my worship, my life and my death are for the sake of God, the Lord of all the nations. He has no partner, and I have been commanded to follow this creed, and I am the first of those who submit to God.' (6:162-163)

☐ He is the Living One, there is no god except Him. So supplicate Him, putting exclusive faith in Him. All praise belongs to God, Lord of all the nations. (40:65)

☐ Indeed, the hypocrites will be in the lowest reach of the Fire, and you will never find any helper for them, except for those who repent and reform and hold fast to God and dedicate their religion exclusively to God. Those are with the faithful, and soon God will give the faithful a great reward. (4:145-146)

Prayer and Fasting

Prayer is a longstanding tradition in the Hebrew Bible, which describes Abraham (Gen. 17:3, 24:52), Moses (Exodus 34:8), Joshua (Josh. 5:14), David (Psalms 119:164), Daniel (Daniel 6:10) and Ezra (Nehemiah 8:1) as offering prayers.

Prayer and fasting are practiced differently by Jews and Christians. Observant Jews pray three times a day, morning, afternoon and evening (*Shacharit, Mincha,* and *Ma'ariv*), with lengthier services on special days, such as Sabbath and Jewish holidays. The Shema Yisrael ("Hear O Israel,"Deuteronomy 6:4-) and the Amidah ("the standing prayer," a Talmudic text) are their most important prayer-texts. The Siddur, a prayerbook used by Jews, contains daily prayers as well as texts for special days and holidays. Their major fasting days are Yom Kippur and 9th of the month of Av (*Tisha B'Av*). Observant Jews fast six days of the year. Moreover, one-year and three-year lectionaries prescribe public readings of the Torah and parts of other prophetic books by the Jewish faithful.

What Christianity lacks in the way of law is made up by its rich liturgical traditions, at least in the Catholic, Orthodox and some Protestant traditions, which have elaborate books of liturgy for daily services, seasons and days. The ancient practice of praying during the 7 or 8 canonical hours[1] had its roots in Psalm, where David says, "Seven times a day I praise you for your righteous laws." The Second Vatican Council, modified the number of the prayers, with four major offices being mandated (Matins, Lauds, Vespers, and Compline), with priests given the choice from among one or more of Terce, Sext, and None as part of mandatory daytime prayer.

Lent is the traditional fasting time in Christianity, a 40-day period in preparation for Easter and commemorating the 40 days Jesus spent fasting in the wilderness. The season is observed in the Roman Catholic, Eastern Orthodox, Oriental Orthodox, Anglican, Lutheran, Methodist, Moravian, Reformed as well as some Anabaptist and evangelical churches. Many Protestant groups do not include fasting as one of their rituals.

---

[1] Lauds - at dawn, Prime - at ~6 am, Terce - at ~9 am, Sext - at ~12 noon, None - at ~3 pm, Vespers - at ~6 pm, Compline - at ~9 pm, Matins - during the night)

'Prayer' (as different from acts of supplicating and making petitions to God) in Islam is a structured performance involving recitations from the Qur'an and kneeling and prostrating to express humility. Prayer and fasting are among the most important obligations which represent the rites of worship in the Islamic faith. Muslims should observe daily prayers and fast during the month of Ramaḍān, as detailed in the books on rites. The Holy Qur'an attaches great importance to these two observances and invites people to perform them punctually, while pointing out some of their beneficial effects.

☐ Maintain the prayer at the two ends of the day, and during the early hours of the night. Indeed, good deeds efface misdeeds. That is an admonition for the mindful. (11:114)

☐ Be watchful of your prayers, and [especially] the middle prayer,[1] and stand devoutly before God. (2:238)

☐ Recite what has been revealed to you of the Book and maintain the prayer. The prayer indeed restrains from indecent and wrongful conduct, and remembrance of God is surely greater. God knows whatever deeds you do. (20:14)

☐ Take recourse in patience and prayer, and it is indeed hard except for the humble—those who are certain they will encounter their Lord and that they will return to Him. (2:45-46)

☐ Tell My servants who have faith to maintain the prayer and to spend secretly and openly from what We have provided them before there comes a day on which there will be neither any bargaining nor friendship. (14:31)

☐ Indeed, those who recite the Book of God and maintain the prayer, and spend secretly and openly out of what We have provided them, expect a commerce that will never go bankrupt,

---

[1] That is, the noon prayer.

so that He may pay them their full reward and enhance them out of His bounty. He is indeed all-forgiving, all-appreciative. (35:29-30)

☐ O you who have faith! Take recourse in patience and prayer; indeed God is with the patient. (2:153)

☐ The righteous will be in gardens, questioning the guilty: 'What drew you into Hell?' They will answer, 'We were not among those who prayed. Nor did we feed the poor. We used to indulge in profane gossip along with the gossipers, and we used to deny the Day of Retribution until death came to us.' (74:40-47)

☐ O you who have faith! Prescribed for you is fasting as was prescribed for those who were before you, so that you may be Godwary. That for known days. But should any of you be sick or on a journey, let it be a similar number of other days. Those who find it straining shall be liable to atonement by feeding a needy person. Should anyone do good of his own accord, that is better for him, and to fast is better for you, should you know. (2:183-184)

☐ The month of Ramadān is one in which the Qur'an was sent down as guidance to mankind, with manifest proofs of guidance and the Criterion. So let those of you who witness it fast in it, and as for someone who is sick or on a journey, let it be a similar number of other days. God desires ease for you, and He does not desire hardship for you, and so that you may complete the number, and magnify God for guiding you, and that you may give thanks. (2:185)

☐ Indeed, the *muslim* men and the *muslim* women, the faithful men and the faithful women, the obedient men and the obedient women, the truthful men and the truthful women, the patient men and the patient women, the humble men and the humble women, the charitable men and the charitable women, the men who fast and the women who fast, the men who guard their private parts and the women who guard, the men who remember God much and the women who remember God much—God holds in store for them forgiveness and a great reward. (33:35)

Zakāt and Khums

Alongside prayer and fasting there are other obligations, including financial ones, namely, payment of *zakāt* and *khums* (a one-fifth), which become due under certain conditions described in books on ritual law. The following verses, besides encouraging the faithful to spend on charities and pay *zakāt* and *khums*, also state the purpose for which they are to be spent. Those who amass riches and do not spend it on charity and other worthy causes are threatened with a dire punishment.

- Indeed, those who have faith, do righteous deeds, maintain the prayer and give the *zakāt*, they shall have their reward near their Lord, and they will have no fear, nor will they grieve. (2:277)

- The charities are only for the poor and the needy and those employed to collect them, and those whose hearts are to be reconciled, and for the freedom of the slaves and the debtors, and to be spent in the way of God, and for the traveller. This is an ordinance from God, and God is all-knowing, all-wise. (9:60)

- Those who persevere in their prayers and there is a known share in whose wealth for the beggar and the deprived, (70:23-25)

- Know that whatever thing you may come by, a fifth of it is for God and the Apostle, for the relatives and the orphans, for the needy and the traveller, if you have faith in God and what We sent down to Our servant on the Day of Separation, the day when the two hosts met; and God has power over all things. (8:41)

◻ Give the relatives their due right, and the needy and the traveller as well, but do not squander wastefully. The wasteful are indeed brothers of satans, and Satan is ungrateful to his Lord. (17:26-27)

◻ Take charity from their possessions to cleanse them and purify them thereby, and bless them. Your blessing is indeed a comfort to them, and God is all-hearing, all-knowing. (9:103)

◻ Struggle for the sake of God, with a struggle which is worthy of Him. He has chosen you and has not placed for you any obstacle in the religion, the faith of your father, Abraham. He named you '*muslims*' before, and in this, so that the Apostle may be a witness to you, and that you may be witnesses to mankind. So maintain the prayer, give the *zakāt*, and hold fast to God. He is your Master—an excellent master and an excellent helper. (22:78)

◻ Those who treasure up gold and silver, and do not spend it in the way of God, inform them of a painful punishment on the day when these shall be heated in hellfire and therewith branded on their foreheads, their sides and their backs and told: 'This is what you treasured up for yourselves! So taste what you have treasured!' (9:34-35)

The Kaʿbah and the Holy Mosque

The Kaʿbah and the Holy Mosque in Mecca have a central place in the sacred geography of Islam. According to Islamic belief, the Kaʿbah was the earliest 'House of God' marked out for the people, and first inaugurated by Abraham and Ishmael, the patriarchs of the Arabs and the Israelites. The offering of sacrifices during the annual pilgrimage to this holy place was a rite that had been practised by Arabs since pre-Islamic times to celebrate Abraham's sacrifice of his first-born son, Ishmael.[1]

However, during the first thirteen years of the Prophet's stay in Mecca and for more than a year after his migration to Medina, the Muslims, continuing the tradition of the authentic followers of the religion of Moses and Jesus, used to pray facing in the direction of Jerusalem, where the Temple first built by Solomon had once stood. The Temple in Jerusalem (בֵּית־הַמִקְדָּשׁ: *Beit Ha-Miqdash*), had itself replaced the Tabernacle, a portable tent first set up by Moses and Aaron as the house of worship for the Israelites during their wanderings in the wilderness. Destroyed by the Babylonians and rebuilt after its first destruction by the returning exiles, it served as Judaism's central place of worship, managed by legions of priests and visited by the devout from all over Palestine and other Jewish colonies during yearly festivals and other occasions.[2]

---

[1] Some Islamic traditions state that 'every beast that is slaughtered at Mina during the rites of Hajj until the Day of Resurrection, is a ransom offering (*fidyah*) for Ishmael' (فكل ما يذبح في منى فهو فدية لإسماعيل إلى يوم القيامة). *'Uyun akhbar al-Rida*, vol. 1, p. 210, bab 18, hadith no. 1, whence *Bihar al-anwar*, vol. 12, pp. 122-123, hadith no. 1 & vol. 15, p. 128, hadith no. 69.

[2] The Temple's history begins bout a thousand years after Abraham and with the origins of the monarchy in the 10th century B.C.E., when it was constructed as a substitute for the portable Tent of Meeting by King Solomon. It was destroyed by the Babylonians, who invaded Judah under Nebuchadnezzar in 587. After nearly seventy years of desolation in the wake of the Babylonian conquest, it was rebuilt under Persian rule after the return of the Jews from Exile, beginning in 520 B.C.E.. A second, enormous rebuilding effort took place under King Herod (37-4 B.C.E.) as part of his extensive building projects, before its final destruction by the Romans in 70 C.E.

☐ Indeed, the first house to be set up for mankind is the one at Bakkah[1], blessed and a guidance for all nations. In it are manifest signs and Abraham's Station, and whoever enters it shall be secure. And it is the duty of mankind toward God to make pilgrimage to the House—for those who can afford the journey to it—and should anyone renege [on his obligation], God is indeed without need of the nations. (3:96-97)

☐ As Abraham raised the foundations of the House with Ishmael, [they prayed]: 'Our Lord, accept it from us! Indeed, You are the All-hearing, the All-knowing. 'Our Lord, make us submissive to You, and [raise] a nation submissive to You from our progeny, show us our rites [of worship], and turn to us clemently. Indeed, You are the All-clement, the All-merciful.' 'Our Lord, raise amongst them an apostle from among them, who will recite to them Your signs and teach them the Book and wisdom, and purify them. Indeed, You are the All-mighty, the All-wise.'(2:127-129)

The Rites of Hajj

One of the most important obligations in Islam is performing the Hajj pilgrimage. It is obligatory on every Muslim if he/she is financially and physically able to travel to Mecca to perform the *hajj* pilgrimage during specific days of the lunar year. The rites of *hajj*, such as assumption of *ihrām* (i.e. the state of pilgrim sanctity) *tawāf* (circuiting the Ka'bah), *sa'y* (going to and fro between Safā and Marwah, which are locations inside the Holy Mosque complex), prayer, and several other rites are detailed in the books on the rites of *hajj*.

☐ Complete the *hajj* and the '*umrah*[2] for God's sake, and

---

[1] An old name for Mecca.
[2] '*Umra*h consists of the particular rites of visit to the Ka'bah, usually

if you are prevented (from access to the Holy Mosque), then make such sacrificial offering as is feasible. And do not shave your heads until the offering reaches its assigned place. But should any of you be sick, or have a hurt in his head, let the atonement be by fasting, or charity, or sacrifice. And when you have security—for those who enjoy release from the restrictions by virtue of their *'umrah* until the *hajj*—let the offering be such as is feasible. (2:196)

☐ As for someone who cannot afford the offering, let him fast three days during the *hajj* and seven when you return; that is a period of ten complete days. That is for someone whose family does not dwell by the Holy Mosque. And be wary of God, and know that God is severe in retribution.

The *hajj* season is in months well-known; so whoever decides on *hajj* pilgrimage therein, should know that there is to be no sexual contact, vicious talk, or disputing during the *hajj*. Whatever good you do, God knows it. And take provision, for Godwariness is indeed the best provision. So be wary of Me, O you who possess intellects!

There is no sin upon you in seeking your Lord's bounty (by way of trade) during the *hajj* season. Then when you stream out of 'Arafāt remember God at the Holy Mashʿar, and remember Him as He has guided you, and earlier you were indeed among the astray.

Then stream out from where the people stream out, and plead to God for forgiveness; indeed God is all-forgiving, all-merciful. And when you finish your rites, remember God as you would remember your fathers, or with a more ardent remembrance. (2:196-200)

☐ When We settled for Abraham the site of the House, saying, Do not ascribe any partners to Me, and purify My House for those who circle around it and those who stand in

---

carried out outside of the *hajj* season.

it for prayer and those who bow and prostrate themselves. And proclaim the *hajj* to all the people: they will come to you on foot and on lean camels, coming from distant places, that they may witness the benefits for them, and mention God's Name during the known days over the livestock He has provided them. So eat thereof, and feed the destitute and the needy. Then let them do away with their untidiness,c fulfil their vows, and circle around the Ancient House. (22:26-29)

☐ Safā and Marwah are indeed among God's sacraments. So whoever makes *hajj* to the House, or performs the '*umrah*, there is no sin upon him to circuit between them. Should anyone do good of his own accord, then God is indeed appreciative, all-knowing. (2:158)

Goodness to Parents

Another obligation is respect for the rights of the parents. One should always be in the service of one's parents and obey them and not offend them. Of course, if they want their child to do something wrong, they should not be obeyed, but at the same time one ought to treat them with respect.

☐ Your Lord has decreed that you shall not worship anyone except Him, and He has enjoined kindness to parents. Should any of them or both reach old age at your side, do not say to them, 'Fie!'[1] And do not chide them, but speak to them noble words. Lower the wing of humility to them mercifully, and say, 'My Lord! Have mercy on them, just as they reared me when I was a small child!' (17:23-24)

☐ We have enjoined man concerning his parents: His mother carried him through weakness upon weakness, and his weaning takes two years. Give thanks to Me and to your parents.

---

[1] An interjection used to express exasperation, distaste or disapproval.

To Me is the return. (31:14)

☐ We have enjoined man to be kind to his parents. His mother has carried him in travail and bore him in travail, and his gestation and weaning take thirty months. When he comes of age and reaches forty years, he says, 'My Lord! Inspire me to give thanks for Your blessing with which You have blessed me and my parents, and that I may do righteous deeds which please You, and invest my descendants with righteousness. I have indeed turned to you in penitence, and I am one of those who have submitted to You.' (46:15)

The Rights of Neighbours and Relatives

One of the social norms recommended in the Qur'an is respect for neighbours and relatives and their rights, so much so that kindness towards relatives and neighbours is placed next to the worship of God. Also, observing the rights of one's relatives is considered a signs of faith and their violation as one of the traits of the losers.

Among precepts to be observed concerning the treatment of neighbours are: not to intrude into the privacy of their homes and not to spare any neighbourly help.

☐ Worship God and do not ascribe any partners to Him, and be good to parents, the relatives, the orphans, the needy, the near neighbour and the distant neighbour, the companion at your side, the traveller, and your slaves. God indeed does not like those who are arrogant and boastful. (4:36)

☐ O you who have faith! Do not enter houses other than your own until you have announced your arrival and greeted their occupants. That is better for you. Maybe you will take admonition. But if you do not find anyone in them, do not enter them until you are given permission. And if you are told: 'Turn back,' then do turn back. That will be more decent on your part. God knows best what you do. (24:27-28)

☐ If the hypocrites and those in whose hearts is a sickness, and the rumourmongers in the city do not desist, We will prompt you to take action against them; then they will not be your neighbours in it except briefly. (33:60)

☐ Woe to those who pray but are heedless of their prayers —who show off but deny neighbourly aid. (107:5-7)

War and Peace

The first principle in Islam is peace, tolerance and peaceful coexistence. War and violence are not desirable unless they become necessary. There are times when there is no other option than war. From the viewpoint of the Qur'an, peace is better than war, but if war with the enemy is necessary, it must be fought with all power and in the cause of God. The defence of the Muslim community and Islamic territories is mandatory and the Qur'an commands Muslims to provide as much military power and equipment as they can to deter the enemies, and to negotiate peace if the enemy calls for it.

☐ Those who are fought against are permitted to fight because they have been wronged, and God is indeed able to help them—those who were expelled from their homes unjustly only because they said, 'God is our Lord.' Had not God repulsed the people from one another, ruin would have befallen the monasteries, churches, synagogues and mosques in which God's Name is much invoked. God will surely help those who help Him. God is indeed all-strong, all-mighty. (22:39-40)

☐ But if they (i.e., the polytheists of Mecca, who had made a treaty with the Muslims after waging a war against them and fighting three battles) break their pledges after their having made a treaty and revile your religion, then fight the leaders of unfaith—indeed they have no commitment to pledges—maybe they will desist.

Will you not make war on a people who broke their pledges and resolved to expel the Apostle, and opened hostilities against you initially? Do you fear them? But God is worthier of being feared by you, should you be faithful. (9:12-13)

- Fight in the way of God those who fight you, but do not transgress. Indeed, God does not like transgressors. (2:190)

- Not equal are those of the faithful who sit back—excepting those who suffer from some disability—and those who wage *jihād* in the way of God with their possession and persons. God has graced those who wage *jihād* with their possessions and persons by a degree over those who sit back; yet to each God has promised the best reward, and God has graced those who wage *jihād* over those who sit back with a great reward: (4:95)

- Go forth, whether armed lightly or heavily, and wage *jihād* with your possessions and persons in the way of God. That is better for you, should you know. (9:41)

- The faithful are only those who have attained faith in God and His Apostle and then have never doubted, and who wage *jihād* with their possessions and their persons in the way of God. It is they who are the truthful. (49:15)

- As for those who strive in Us, We shall surely guide them in Our ways, and God is indeed with the virtuous. (29:69)

- Prepare against them whatever you can of military power and war-horses, awing thereby the enemy of God and your enemy, and others besides them, whom you do not know, but God knows them. And whatever you spend in the way of God will be repaid to you in full and you will not be wronged. If they incline toward peace, you too incline toward it and put your trust in God. Indeed, He is the All-hearing, the All-knowing.

But if they desire to deceive you, God is indeed sufficient for you. It is He who strengthened you with His help and with the means of the faithful, (8:60-62)

☐ Do not suppose those who were slain in the way of God to be dead; no, they are living and provided for near their Lord, exulting in what God has given them out of His grace, and rejoicing for those who have not yet joined them from those left behind them, that they will have no fear, nor will they grieve. They rejoice in God's blessing and grace, and that God does not waste the reward of the faithful. (3:169-171)

☐ Do not call those who were slain in God's way 'dead.' No, they are living, but you are not aware. (2:154)

☐ Then their Lord answered them, 'I do not waste the work of any worker among you, whether male or female; you are all on the same footing. So those who migrated and were expelled from their homes, and were tormented in My way, and those who fought and were killed—I will surely absolve them of their misdeeds and I will admit them into gardens with streams running in them, as a reward from God, and God—with Him is the best of rewards.' (3:195)

Fulfilment of Vows and Oaths

One of the obligations of a Muslim is that when he/she makes a vow or covenant or takes an oath, meeting certain conditions, he/she must perform it or else he/she has sinned and is required to make an atonement.

Fulfilment of covenant and vow is one of the praiseworthy attributes commanded in the Qur'anic verses.

☐ Fulfil God's covenant when you pledge, and do not break your oaths after pledging them solemnly and having made God a witness over yourselves. God indeed knows what you do. (16:91)

☐ Indeed, the pious will drink from a cup seasoned with *Kāfūr*, a spring where God's servants will drink, making it gush forth as they please. They fulfil their vows and fear a day whose ill will be widespread. (76:6-7)

☐ God indeed knows whatever charity you may give, or vows that you may vow, and the wrongdoers have no helpers. (2:270)

☐ Only those who possess intellect take admonition—those who fulfil God's covenant and do not break the pledge solemnly made, and those who join what God has commanded to be joined, fear their Lord, and are afraid of an adverse reckoning. (13:20-21)

☐ God will not take you to task for what is frivolous in your oaths; but He will take you to task for what you pledge in earnest. The atonement for it is to feed ten needy persons with the average food you give to your families, or their clothing, or the freeing of a slave. He who cannot afford any of these shall fast for three days. That is the atonement for your oaths when you vow. But keep your oaths. Thus does God clarify His signs for you so that you may give thanks. (5:89)

Observance of Modesty and Norms of Decency

Islam has special rules for ensuring the moral health of the community and security of the family, which if observed will prevent moral corruption and deviation. One of them is the issue of modest clothing and manners, which has a great role on both strengthening the family's foundations and saving young people from waywardness. The Qur'an states that the purpose of the veil for women is to maintain their dignity and protect them from harms that arise from degenerate social customs. These issues are explicitly addressed in this verse.

☐ Tell the faithful men to cast down their looks and to guard their private parts. That is more decent for them. God is indeed well aware of what they do. And tell the faithful women to cast down their looks and to guard their private parts, and not to display their charms, beyond what is acceptably visible, and let them draw their scarfs over their bosoms, and not display their charms except to their husbands, or their fathers, or their husband's fathers, or their sons, or their husband's sons, or their brothers, or their brothers' sons, or their sisters' sons, or their women, or their slave girls, or male dependants lacking [sexual] desire, or children uninitiated to women's intimate parts. And let them not thump their feet to make known their hidden ornaments[1]. Rally to God in repentance, O faithful, so that you may be felicitous. (24:30-31)

☐ O Prophet! Tell your wives and your daughters and the women of the faithful to draw closely over themselves their *chadors* when going out. That makes it likely for them to be recognized and not be troubled, and God is all-forgiving, all-merciful. (33:59)

☐ O you who have faith! Your slaves and those of you who have not yet reached puberty should seek your permission at three times: before the dawn prayer, and when you put off your garments at noon, and after the night prayer. These are three times of privacy for you. Apart from these, it is not sinful of you or them to frequent one another freely. Thus does God clarify the signs for you, and God is all-knowing, all-wise. (24:58)

☐ … Those who guard their private parts—except from their spouses and their slave women, for then they are not blameworthy; but whoever seeks beyond that it is they who are the transgressors—and those who keep their trusts and covenants, and those who are conscientious in their testimonies, and those who are watchful of their prayers. (70:29-35)

---

[1] Such as ankle chains and bracelets.

CHAPTER 11

Religious Prohibitions

Polytheism and Hypocrisy

Carving up peers and partners for God, fabricating false deities, and associating others with Him in worship is regarded as polytheism (*shirk*) and is the greatest sin which will not be forgiven. So is 'hypocrisy' (*nifāq*), which means not believing in God but pretending to do so. The place of polytheists and hypocrites who do not repent is hell.

☐ Indeed, God does not forgive that a partner should be ascribed to Him, but He forgives anything besides that to whomever He wishes. Whoever ascribes partners to God has indeed fabricated a lie in great sinfulness. (4:48)

☐ Say (O Prophet), 'I am just a human being like you. It has been revealed to me that your God is the One God. So whoever expects to encounter his Lord, let him act righteously and not associate anyone with the worship of his Lord.' (18:110)

☐ Say, 'My Lord has forbidden only indecencies, the outward among them and the inward ones, and sin and undue aggression, and that you should ascribe to God partners for which He has not sent down any authority, and that you should attribute to God what you do not know.' (7:33)

☐ Say, 'All praise belongs to God, who has neither any

offspring, nor has He any partner in sovereignty, nor has He made any friend out of weakness,' and magnify Him with a magnification worthy of Him. (17:111)

☐ So set your heart as a person of pure faith on this religion, the original nature endowed by God, according to which He originated mankind (There is no altering God's creation; that is the upright religion, but most people do not know)—turning to Him in penitence, and be wary of Him, and maintain the prayer, and do not be one of the polytheists—those who split up their religion and became sects: each faction boasting about what it possessed. (30:30-32)

☐ God will surely punish the hypocrites, men and women, and the polytheists, men and women, and God will turn clemently to the faithful, men and women, and God is all-forgiving, all-merciful. (33:73)

☐ Inform the hypocrites that there is a painful punishment for them—those who take the faithless for allies instead of the faithful. Do they seek honour with them? If so, all honour belongs to God (4:138-139)

☐ Indeed, the hypocrites will be in the lowest reach of the Fire, and you will never find any helper for them, (4:145)

☐ The hypocrites, men and women, are all alike: they bid what is wrong and forbid what is right, and are tight-fisted. They have forgotten God, so He has forgotten them. The hypocrites are indeed the transgressors. God has promised the hypocrites, men and women, and the faithless, the Fire of hell, to remain in it. That suffices them. God has cursed them, and there is a lasting punishment for them. (9:67-68)

☐ When the hypocrites come to you (O Prophet), they say, 'We bear witness that you are indeed the apostle of God.' God knows that you are indeed His Apostle, and God bears witness that the hypocrites are indeed liars. They make a shield of their oaths and bar from the way of God. Evil indeed is what they have been doing. (63:1-2)

Homicide

After *shirk* and hypocrisy, the greatest sin is homicide. From the viewpoint of the Qur'an, killing an innocent person is like killing all human beings. Whoever deliberately murders an innocent person goes out of the pale of the religion of God and will stay in hell forever.

The heirs of the victim are allowed to take retribution and to slay the killer. At the same time, it is better that they renounce their right and forgive the murderer. However, retaliation serves as a deterrent and prevents much violence and killings and in fact gives life to society.

☐ Should anyone kill a believer intentionally, his requital shall be hell, to remain in it; God shall be wrathful at him and curse him and He will prepare for him a great punishment. (4:93)

☐ That is why We decreed for the Children of Israel that whoever kills a soul, without its being guilty of manslaughter or corruption on the earth, is as though he had killed all mankind, and whoever saves a life is as though he had saved all mankind. Our apostles certainly brought them clear signs, yet even after that many of them commit excesses on the earth. (5:32)

☐ A believer may not kill another believer, unless it is by mistake. Anyone who kills a believer by mistake should set free a believing slave and pay blood-money to his family, unless they remit it in charity. If he belongs to a people who are hostile to you but is a believer, then a believing slave is to be set free. And if he belongs to a people with whom you have a treaty, the blood-money is to be paid to his family and a believing slave is to be set free. He who does not afford freeing a slave must fast for two successive months as a penance from God, and God is all-knowing, all-wise. (4:92)

☐ Do not kill a soul whose life God has made inviolable, except with due cause, and whoever is killed wrongfully, We have certainly given his heir an authority. But let him not commit any excess in killing, for he enjoys the support of law. (17:33)

☐ There is life for you in retribution, O you who possess intellects! Maybe you will be Godwary! (2:179)

☐ Say, '… You shall not approach indecencies, the outward among them and the inward ones, and you shall not kill a soul whose life God has made inviolable, except with due cause. This is what He has enjoined upon you so that you may exercise your reason. (6:151)

Illicit Gains

There is nothing wrong with trying to obtain wealth legitimately and using it properly; rather it is something desirable. But obtaining wealth through illicit means and using it has far-reaching evil consequences for one's life and family. Consumption of illicit income deprives one of life's true blessings and darkens one's understanding. Some instances of illicit gains are mentioned in the Qur'an, including misappropriating the property of orphans, usurping others' property and belongings, consuming wealth obtained through bribery, fraudulent dealings and trade malpractices, gambling, usury, theft, and other illicit means.

☐ Do not eat up your wealth among yourselves wrongfully, nor proffer it to the judges in order to eat up a part of the people's wealth sinfully, while you know that it is immoral to do so. (2:188)

☐   O you who have faith! Do not eat up your wealth among yourselves unrightfully, but it should be trade by mutual consent. And do not kill yourselves. Indeed, God is most merciful to you. And whoever does that in aggression and injustice, We will soon make him enter the Fire, and that is easy for God. (4:29-30)

☐   O you who have faith! Do not exact usury, twofold and severalfold, and be wary of God so that you may be felicitous. Beware of the Fire which has been prepared for the faithless, (3:130-131)

☐   Those who exact usury will not stand but like one deranged by the Devil's touch. That is because they say, 'Trade is just like usury.' While God has allowed trade and forbidden usury. Whoever relinquishes usury on receiving advice from his Lord shall keep the gains of what is past, and his matter will rest with God. As for those who resume, they shall be the inmates of the Fire and they will remain in it. (2:275)

☐   Deliver to the orphans their property, and do not replace the good with the bad, and do not eat up their property by mingling it with your own property, for that is indeed a great sin. (4:2)

☐   Those who consume the property of orphans wrongfully, only ingest fire into their bellies, and soon they will enter the Blaze. (4:10)

☐   O you who have faith! Indeed, many of the (Jewish) scribes and (Christian) monks wrongfully eat up the people's wealth, and bar them from the way of God. Those who treasure up gold and silver, and do not spend it in the way of God, inform them of a painful punishment on the day when these shall be heated in hellfire and therewith branded on their foreheads, their sides and their backs and told: 'This is what you treasured up for yourselves! So taste what you have treasured!' (9:34-35)

☐   Why do not the rabbis and the scribes forbid them from sinful speech and consuming illicit gains? Surely, evil is what they have been working. (5:63)

Defamation and Lying

Of the major sins that result from abuse of speech is lying and slandering innocent persons. The worst kind of slander is attributing falsehoods to God and His prophets. Fabrication of lies has been identified in the Qur'an as the main source of corruption of religious teachings.

To accuse someone falsely of an ugly deed and to spoil his or her reputation is a flagrant and unforgivable sin and one of the ugliest acts. From the Qur'an's point of view, those who lie and slander are persons who do not believe in the revelations of God. The liar and fabricator of lies is a wrongdoer and is deprived of salvation.

☐   Only those fabricate lies who do not believe in the signs of God, and it is they who are the liars. (16:105)

☐   Do not say, asserting falsely with your tongues, 'This is lawful, and that is unlawful,' attributing lies to God. Indeed, those who attribute lies to God will not prosper. (16:116)

☐   Who is a greater wrongdoer than him who fabricates lies against God or denies His signs? Indeed, the wrongdoers will not be felicitous. (6:21)

☐   Say (O Prophet), 'Have you regarded what God has sent down for you of His provision, whereupon you have made some of it unlawful and some lawful?' Say, 'Did God give you the sanction to do so, or do you fabricate lies against God?' What is the idea of those who fabricate lies against God concerning their own situation on the Day of Resurrection? God is indeed gracious to mankind, but most of them do not give thanks. (10:59-60)

☐ O Prophet! If faithful women come to you to take the oath of allegiance to you, pledging that they shall not ascribe any partners to God, that they shall not steal, nor commit adultery, nor kill their children, nor produce a lie that they may have hatched between their hands and feet, nor disobey you in what is right, then accept their allegiance and plead for them to God for forgiveness. God is indeed all-forgiving, all-merciful. (60:12)

☐ Indeed, those who accuse chaste and unwary faithful women shall be cursed in this world and the Hereafter, and there shall be a great punishment for them. (24:23)

☐ Whoever commits an iniquity or sin and then accuses an innocent person of it, is indeed guilty of calumny and a flagrant sin. (4:112)

Backbiting, Vilification, Suspicion, and Spying

Speaking ill of someone in his absence and mentioning his weak points when he is not present to defend himself is called backbiting, which is a gross sin. The ugliness of backbiting is so great that according to the Qur'an that one who speaks ill of someone in his absence is likened to one who eats the flesh of that person. Vilification, suspicion, and curiosity to find others' faults are also in the same category as backbiting, and someone who has these vile traits and seeks to discredit others, is guilty of a major sin.

☐ O you who have faith! Avoid much suspicion; some suspicions are indeed sins. And do not spy on one another or backbite. Will any of you love to eat the flesh of his dead brother? You would hate it. Be wary of God; God is indeed all-clement, all-merciful. (49:12)

☐ God does not like the disclosure of anyone's evil conduct

in speech except by someone who has been wronged, and God is all-hearing, all-knowing. (4:148)

◻ Indeed, those who want indecency to spread among the faithful—there is a painful punishment for them in the world and the Hereafter, and God knows and you do not know. (24:19)

◻ O you who have faith! Let not any people ridicule another people: it may be that they are better than they are; nor let women ridicule women: it may be that they are better than they are. And do not defame one another, nor insult one another by calling nicknames. How evil are profane names subsequent to faith! As for those who are not repentant of their past conduct—they are the wrongdoers. (49:11)

Adultery and Prostitution

Illegal sexual relations cause a great deal of personal and social harm, and result in spreading corruption and indecency, disrupting family relations and lineages. Regarded as a major sin they are severely prohibited in the Holy Qur'an.

According to these verses, the fornicators and adulterers, men and women, must be punished. Adultery is a very ugly form of indecency and as it is on a par with idolatry and homicide, the faithful have been warned from even approaching it, which means that one should avoid things that may lead to adultery.

◻ Do not approach fornication. It is indeed an indecency and an evil way. (17:32)

◻ As for the fornicatress and the fornicator, strike each of them a hundred lashes, and let not pity for them overcome you in God's law, if you believe in God and the Last Day, and let their punishment be witnessed by a group of the faithful. (24:2)

☐ Those who do not invoke another deity besides God, and do not kill a soul whose life God has made inviolable, except with due cause, and do not commit fornication. Whoever does that shall encounter its retribution, the punishment being doubled for him on the Day of Resurrection. (25:68)

☐ Should any of your women commit an indecent act, produce against them four witnesses from yourselves, and if they testify, detain them in their houses until death finishes them, or God decrees a course for them. (4:15)

☐ And Lot, when he said to his people, 'What! Do you commit this indecency while you look on? Do you approach men with sexual desire instead of women?! You are indeed an ignorant lot!' (27:54-55)

Wine and Gambling

In Islam all kinds of intoxicants including alcohol are strongly prohibited. The harms of alcohol have been recognized since ancient times and in a recent study scientists have warned that there is no safe level of drinking alcohol when it comes to preserving our health.[1] Gambling is a ruinous and toxic practice that has many detrimental financial, moral and social consequences. The Holy Qur'an describes gambling, drinking of wine and divination as Satanic practices that must be avoided.

☐ O you who have faith! Indeed, wine, gambling, idols and the divining arrows are abominations of Satan's doing, so avoid them, so that you may be felicitous. Indeed, Satan seeks to cast enmity and hatred among you through wine and gambling, and to hinder you from the remembrance of God and from prayer. Will you, then, relinquish? (5:90-91)

---

[1] https://www.thelancet.com/article/S0140-6736(18)31571-X/fulltext

☐   They ask you (O Prophet) concerning wine and gambling. Say, 'There is a great sin in both of them, and some profits for the people, but their sinfulness outweighs their profit.' (2:219)

☐   O you who have faith! Do not approach prayer when you are intoxicated, not until you know what you are saying. (4:43)

Theft, Banditry and Terrorism

Theft is one of the major crimes that is considered heinous and abominable in all societies. The most severe kind of it is banditry and armed robbery, which the Qur'an likens to waging a war against God and His Apostle and 'causing corruption on earth.'

The punishment of the thief, when theft occurs under certain conditions, is to cut off his hand and this is a kind of deterrent. Also, bandits and terrorists, who in addition to stealing people's property create insecurity, are to be punished more severely.

☐   As for the thief, man or woman, cut off their hands as a requital for what they have earned. That is an exemplary punishment from God, and God is all-mighty, all-wise. But whoever repents after his wrongdoing and reforms, God shall accept his repentance. God is indeed all-forgiving, all-merciful. (5:38-39)

☐   Indeed, the requital of those who wage war against God and His Apostle, and try to cause corruption in the land, is that they shall be slain or crucified, or shall have their hands and feet cut off on opposite sides, or be banished from the land. That is a disgrace for them in this world, and there is a great punishment for them in the Hereafter, excepting those who repent before you capture them, and know that God is all-forgiving, all-merciful. (5:33-34)

☐ Among the people is he whose talk about worldly life impresses you, and he holds God witness to what is in his heart, though he is the staunchest of enemies. If he were to wield authority, he would try to cause corruption in the land and to ruin the crop and the stock, and God does not like corruption. (2:204-205)

☐ Those who break the covenant made with God after having pledged it solemnly, and sever what God has commanded to be joined, and cause corruption in the land—it is they who are the losers. (2:27)

☐ Shall We treat those who have faith and do righteous deeds like those who cause corruption in the land? Shall We treat the Godwary like the vicious? (38:28)

Pursuit of Base Desires

The cause of many sins is following one's base desires. Base desires lead human beings into situations where they may commit any illegitimate deed and overstep the bounds of law and morality in order to satisfy them. Of course, people possessing faith oppose their base motives in order to avoid sin.

Some follow the dictates of their base desire as if they considered it to be their own god, and this causes them to transgress and commit extreme actions.

☐ Have you seen him who has taken his base desire to be his god? Is it your duty to watch over him? (25:43)

☐ Do not obey him whose heart We have made oblivious to Our remembrance and who follows his base desires, and whose conduct is mere profligacy. (18:28)

☐ But they (i.e., the prophets of old) were succeeded by an evil posterity who neglected the prayer and followed their base appetites. So they will soon encounter the reward of perversity, (19:59)

☐ Then, if they (i.e., the faithless among the Jews) do not respond to your summons, know that they only follow their base desires, and who is more astray than him who follows his base desires without any guidance from God? Indeed, God does not guide the wrongdoing lot. (28:50)

☐ But as for him who is awed to stand before his Lord and restrains his soul from following base desires, his refuge will indeed be paradise. (79:37-41)

☐ They (i.e., the pagan Arabs) follow nothing but conjectures and the base desires of the lower soul, while there has already come to them the guidance from their Lord. (53:23)

☐ Relate to them an account of him[1] to whom We gave Our signs, but he cast them off. Thereupon Satan pursued him, and he became one of the perverse. Had We wished, We would have surely raised him by their means, but he clung to the earth and followed his base desires. So his parable is that of a dog: if you make for it, it lolls out its tongue, and if you let it alone, it lolls out its tongue. Such is the parable of the people who impugn Our signs. So recount these narratives, so that they may reflect. (7:175-176)

Following the Devil

Satan is a creature that stand in the way of human beings to deter them from the right path. This evil character can be a human person who makes others do ugly things, or he can be a genie who with his constant temptations blocks the path of felicity and forces one into rebellion and corrupt ways.

The chief of the devils is Iblis, a Jinn who disobeyed

---

[1] According to one interpretation, this refers to Balaam son of Beor.

God at the time of Adam's creation and was thrown out of the divine court and swore to sit in ambush for Adam's children and mislead them.

The devil and his temptations provide the faithful with the opportunity to achieve spiritual and spiritual excellence by overcoming his efforts and opposing him. That is why the Holy Qur'an has repeatedly called upon the faithful to oppose Satan and declares him an open enemy of mankind.

Satan makes ugly acts appear fair and decorous and creates enmity among the people, and sometimes does so gradually and imperceptibly, step by step.

☐ O you who have faith! Enter into submission, all together, and do not follow in Satan's steps; he is indeed your manifest enemy. (2:208)

☐ O you who have faith! Do not follow in Satan's steps. Whoever follows in Satan's steps should know that he indeed prompts you to commit indecent and wrongful acts. Were it not for God's grace and His mercy upon you, not one of you would ever become pure. But God purifies whomever He wishes, and God is all-hearing, all-knowing. (24:21)

☐ By God, We have certainly sent apostles to nations before you. But Satan made their deeds seem decorous to them. So he is their master today and there is a painful punishment for them. (16:63)

☐ Indeed, those who turned their backs after the guidance had become clear to them, it was Satan who had seduced them and he had given them far-flung hopes. (47:25)

☐ 'Did I not exhort you, O children of Adam, saying, "Do not worship Satan. He is indeed your manifest enemy. Worship Me. That is a straight path"? He has already led astray many of your generations. Did you not exercise your reason? (36:60-62)

☐ Satan has prevailed upon them, so he has caused them to forget the remembrance of God. They are Satan's confederates. Behold, it is Satan's confederates who are indeed the losers! (58:19)

☐ Say, 'My Lord! I seek Your protection from the promptings of devils.' (23:97)

☐ When those who are Godwary are touched by a visitation of Satan, they remember God and, behold, they perceive. But their brethren, they draw them into perversity, and then they do not spare any harm. (7:201-202)

☐ Tell My servants to speak in a manner which is the best. Indeed, Satan incites ill feeling between them, and Satan is indeed man's open enemy. (17:53)☐ Satan frightens you of poverty and prompts you to commit indecent acts. But God promises you His forgiveness and grace, and God is all-bounteous, all-knowing. (2:268)

☐ Those who are themselves stingy and bid other people to be stingy, too, and conceal what God has given them out of His bounty—We have prepared a humiliating punishment for the faithless and those who spend their wealth to be seen by people, and believe neither in God nor in the Last Day. As for him who has Satan for his companion—an evil companion is he! (4:38)

Vicious Conduct and Traits

In Islamic society, Muslims must avoid misconduct and vicious traits. The following verses call for avoiding such conduct as wastefulness, self-conceit, boasting, bullying, mistrust, vilification, detracting, propagation of indecency, immodest glances, ridiculing and harassing others and the like.

☐ O Children of Adam! Put on your adornment on every occasion of prayer, and eat and drink, but do not waste; indeed He does not like the wasteful. (7:31)

☐ Do not turn your cheek away disdainfully from the people, and do not walk boastfully on the earth. Indeed, God does not like any swaggering braggart. Be modest in your bearing, and lower your voice. Indeed, the ungainliest of voices is the donkey's voice.' (31:18-19)

☐ O you who have faith! Avoid much suspicion; some suspicions are indeed sins. And do not spy on one another or backbite. Will any of you love to eat the flesh of his dead brother? You would hate it. Be wary of God; God is indeed all-clement, all-merciful. (49:12)

☐ Those who blame the voluntary donors from among the faithful concerning the charities and ridicule those who do not find anything except what their means permit, God will put them to ridicule and there is a painful punishment for them. (9:79)

☐ Woe to every scandal-monger and slanderer, who amasses wealth and counts it over. He supposes his wealth will make him immortal! (104:01)

☐ Those who took their religion for diversion and play and whom the life of the world had deceived. So today We will forget them as they forgot the encounter of this day of theirs, and used to impugn Our signs. (7:51)

☐ Indeed, those who want indecency to spread among the faithful—there is a painful punishment for them in the world and the Hereafter, and God knows and you do not know. (24:19)

☐ Among the people is he who buys diversionary talk that he may lead people astray from God's way without any knowledge, and he takes it in derision. For such there is a humiliating punishment. (31:6)

☐ O you who have faith! Let not any people ridicule another people: it may be that they are better than they are; nor let women ridicule women: it may be that they are better than they are. And do not defame one another, nor insult one another by calling nicknames. How evil are profane names subsequent to faith! As for those who are not penitent of their past conduct—they are the wrongdoers. (49:11)

☐ Those who offend faithful men and women undeservedly, certainly bear the guilt of slander and flagrant sin. (33:58)

☐ [Malicious] secret talks are indeed from Satan, that he may upset the faithful, but he cannot harm them in any way except by God's leave, and in God alone let all the faithful put their trust. (58:10)

☐ Tell the faithful men to cast down their looks and to guard their private parts. That is more decent for them. God is indeed well aware of what they do. And tell the faithful women to cast down their looks and to guard their private parts, and not to display their charms, beyond what is acceptably visible, and let them draw their scarfs over their bosoms, and not display their charms except to their husbands, or their fathers, or their husband's fathers, or their sons, or their husband's sons, or their brothers, or their brothers' sons, or their sisters' sons, or their women,c or their slave girls, or male dependants lacking [sexual] desire, or children uninitiated to women's intimate parts. And let them not thump their feet to make known their hidden ornaments. Rally to God in repentance, O faithful, so that you may be felicitous. (24:30-31)

☐ Obey God and His Apostle and do not dispute, or you will lose heart and your power will be gone. And be patient; indeed God is with the patient. (8:46)

Attending Sinful Gatherings

Presence in a gathering of people engaged in an activity that amounts to disobeying God and committing sin has a profound effect on the human spirit. The company of the sinful diminishes the ugliness of sin in one's eyes, and may even lead one into sin by the encouragement of those present.

That is why God in the Qur'an warns man against sitting in such a gathering and commands one to leave such assemblies and not to associate with the wrongdoers.

☐   Certainly He has sent down to you in the Book that when you hear God's signs being disbelieved and derided, do not sit with them until they engage in some other discourse, or else you too will be like them. God will indeed gather the hypocrites and the faithless in hell all together. (4:140)

☐   When you see those who gossip impiously about Our signs, avoid them until they engage in some other discourse; but if Satan makes you forget, then, after remembering, do not sit with the wrongdoing lot. (6:68)

☐   To God belong the Best Names, so supplicate Him by them, and abandon those who commit sacrilege in His names. Soon they shall be requited for what they used to do. (7:180)

☐   Those who do not give false testimony, and when they come upon frivolity, pass by with dignity. (25:72)

Index

Ability to Raise the Dead 130
Adam's creation 31
Adultery 215
Afterlife 130
Agreements 189
alcohol 216
anthropomorphism 22
Backbiting 214
Banditry 217
Basis of Belief 13
Belief 13
   Rationality as the Basis of 13
Children of Israel 121123–121 ,
Christians 125
   Qur'anic criticism of 126–128
Cleanliness 176
Communities
   Emergence of Communities 107
Communities and Groups 107
   Non-Muslim Communities 114
Confrontation Between Right and
   Wrong 46
Consultation 189
Cooperation and Teamwork 167
Covenant
   Covenant of the Prophets 54
   With the Israelites 120
Covenant of the Prophets 54
Criterion is Faith and Righteous
   Conduct 115
Day of Resurrection 132
Defamation and Lying 213

Desires 218
Devil 219
Disinformation 172
Divine Help in the Prophet's life 88
Divine Traditions in History 40
Divine Unity 21
Doctrine 11
Doomsday Terror 135
Duty to Urge Rightful & Forbid
   Wrongful Conduct 187
Enemies of the Prophets 64
Eschatology 130
Ethics 85
   Backbiting, Vilification, Suspi-
     cion, and Spying 214
   Cleanliness 176
   Cooperation and Teamwork 167
   Defamation and Lying 213
   Duty to Urge Rightful & Forbid
     Wrongful Conduct 187
   Ethics of the Qur'an 145
   Etiquette of Speaking and Listen-
     ing 172
   Forgiving Others' Trespasses 164
   Gentleness in Behaviour and
     Polite Speech 165
   Greeting Others 175
   Humility 173
   Loving God's Friends 162
   Patience and Perseverance 161
   Respect for Others Privacy 168
   Self-Cultivation and Godwariness

159
Strengthening the Family System 169
Sympathetic Advice 166
Ethics of the Qur'an 145
Etiquette of Speaking and Listening 172
Faith 147
  Faith and Righteous Conduct 147
Faith and Righteous Conduct 147
Faithful, the 108
  Visage of the Faithful 108
Faithless and the Evildoers 111
Faithless, the 108 111 ,
Family 169
Fasting 192
Forgiving Others' Trespasses 164
Freedom 44
Freedom of Choice 44
Fulfilment of Vows and Oaths 205
Gainsayers 64
Gambling 216
Gathering of People at the Resurrection 133
Gatherings 224
Gentleness 165
God 19
  Ability to Raise the Dead 130
  Divine Traditions in History 40
  Existence 19
  Forgiver of Sins 28
  God's Emissaries 50
  God's Envoys 50
  God's Friends 162
  Help to the Prophets 56
  Knowledge of 19
  Names and Attributes 25

Obedience to God and the Apostle 182
Oneness of God 21
Remembrance and Supplication 156
Signs of God's Existence 19
Sincerity and Intent of Nearness to God 190
Thanksgiving 157
  the All-Beneficent and the All-Merciful 26
Trust in God 154
God's Existence 19
God's Help to the Prophets 56
God's Names and Attributes 25
Godwariness 159
Godwary 108
Good Faith 166
Goodness to Parents 201
Greatness of the Qur'an 96
Greeting Others 175
Guidance 101
Hajj 199
Hebrew Bible 70
Hell 142
  Inmates of Hell 142
History 40
  Final End of History 48
Holy Mosque 197
Homicide 210
Human Being 31
  Evolution 36
  God's Viceroy on Earth 31
  Human dignity 35
  Human Life a Test and Trial 38
  Human Nature 34
  in the Qur'an 31
Human dignity 35

Humanity of the Prophets 55
Human Life a Test and Trial 38
Human Nature 34
Humility 173
Hypocrisy 208
Iblis 219
Illicit Gains 211
intoxicants 216
Invitation to Virtues 153
Israelites 120
   Covenant of 120
   Qur'anic criticism of 120
Jesus 125–128
Jews 120
Jews and Christians 118
Justice 185
Ka'bah 197
Knowing God 19
Knowledge 149
Laws of the Qur'an 179
Learning the Laws 183
Loving God's Friends 162
Loyalty to Trusts and Agreements 189
Lying 213
Man on the Path of Evolution 36
Miracles 65
Miracles of the Prophets 65
Mockery and Persecution of the Prophets 60
Modesty 206
Monotheism 21
Moses
   People of 121
Muhammad 68
   Divine Help in the Prophet's life 88
   Names and Titles in the Qur'an 86
   Obligation to Obey the Prophet 89
   Principles of His Invitation 82
   Prophet Muhammad in the Hebrew Bible 70
   Prophet Muhammad in the New Testament 78
   Prophet Muhammad in the Qur'an 81
   Prophet's Morals 85
   Qur'an on the Prophecies in Torah & the Gospel 68
   Spiritual Strengthening of the Prophet 91
   to be Treated with Honour 93
Names and Titles of the Prophet in the Qur'an 86
Neighbours 202
   Rights of 202
New Testament 78
   Prophet Muhammad in the New Testament 78
Non-Muslim Communities 114
   Relations with Non-Muslims 116
Non-Muslims 116
Norms of Decency 206
Oaths 205
Obedience to God and the Apostle 182
Obligations and Ordinances 181
Obligation to Obey the Prophet 89
Paradise 139
   Inhabitants of Paradise 139
Parents 201
   Rights of 201
Patience and Perseverance 161
People of the Book 118

Christians 125
Jews 120
Polite Speech 165
polytheism 22–25
Polytheism 208
Prayer 192
Privacy 168
Prohibitions 208
Prophetic Mission 61
Prophet Muhammad in the Hebrew Bible 70
Prophet Muhammad in the New Testament 78
Prophet Muhammad in the Qur'an 81
Prophets 50
   Attributes of the Prophets 52
   Covenant of the Prophets 54
   Enemies and Gainsayers 64
   God's Help to the Prophets 56
   Humanity of the Prophets 55
   Miracles of 65
   Mockery and Persecution of 60
   Obedience to God and the Apostle 182
   Obligation to Obey the Prophet 89
   Prophetic Mission 61
   Prophet is to be Treated with Honour 93
   Prophets as God's Emissaries 50
   Prophet's Proofs and Arguments 57
   Role of the Prophets 107
   Teachings 62
Prophet's Proofs and Arguments 57
Prostitution 215
Punishments 137

Qur'an, the
   Comprehensiveness of the Qur'an 105
   Confirms the Former Scriptures 103
   Ethics of the Qur'an 145
   Greatness of the Qur'an 96
   Laws of the Qur'an 179
   Names and Titles of the Prophet in the Qur'an 86
   Prophet Muhammad in the Qur'an 81
   Qur'an as Guidance 101
   Recitation of 100
   Revelation of the Qur'an 98
Qur'an, the 96
Rationality 13
Rationality as the Basis of Belief 13
Reason 13
Reason and Revelation 13
Recitation of the Qur'an 100
Reign of the Righteous 48
Reign of the Righteous as the Final End of History 48
Relations with Non-Muslims 116
Relatives 202
   Rights of 202
Religious Prohibitions 208
Remembrance 156
Repentance 151
Respect for Others' Privacy 168
Resurrection 130
   Day of Resurrection 132
   Doomsday Terror 135
   Gathering of People at the Resurrection 133
   God's Ability to Raise the Dead 130

People's State at Resurrection 134
Rewards and Punishments 137
Revelation 1398,
Revelation as the Source of Guidance 14
Revelation of the Qur'an 98
Rewards and Punishments 137
Right and Wrong 46
Righteous Conduct 147
Rights of Neighbours and Relatives 202
Rites of Hajj 199
Role Models 162
Role of God's Envoys 50
Satan 219
Self-Cultivation 159
Signs of God's Existence 19
Sin 151
   Repentance From 151
Sincerity and Intent of Nearness to God 190
Sinful Gatherings 224
Societies
   Factors of their Fall 42
Societies 42
Source of Guidance 14
Speech
   Politeness of 165
Spiritual Strengthening of the Prophet 91
Spying 214
Strengthening the Family System 169
Supplication 156
Suspicion 214
Sympathetic Advice 166
Teachings of the Prophets 62
Terrorism 217

Thanksgiving 157
Theft 217
Traits 221
Trust in God 154
Trusts 189
Unity of the Godhead 21
Values and Norms 147
Vicious Conduct 221
Vilification 214
Virtues 153
Vows 205
War and Peace 203
Wine 216
Works
   Faith and Righteous Conduct 147
Worldview 11
Worship
   Prayer and Fasting 192
   Rites of Hajj 199
   Sincerity and Intent of Nearness to God 190
   Zakāt and Khums 196
Zakāt and Khums 196

www.ingramcontent.com/pod-product-compliance
Lightning Source LLC
LaVergne TN
LVHW041332080426
835512LV00006B/416